Weblogs and Libraries

CHANDOS
INFORMATION PROFESSIONAL SERIES

Series Editor: Ruth Rikowski
(email: rikowski@tiscali.co.uk)

Chandos' new series of books are aimed at the busy information professional. They have been specially commissioned to provide the reader with an authoritative view of current thinking. They are designed to provide easy-to-read and (most importantly) practical coverage of topics that are of interest to librarians and other information professionals. If you would like a full listing of current and forthcoming titles, please visit our web site **www.chandospublishing.com** or contact Hannah Grace-Williams on email info@chandospublishing.com or telephone number +44 (0) 1865 884447.

New authors: we are always pleased to receive ideas for new titles; if you would like to write a book for Chandos, please contact Dr Glyn Jones on email gjones@chandospublishing.com or telephone number +44 (0) 1865 884447.

Bulk orders: some organisations buy a number of copies of our books. If you are interested in doing this, we would be pleased to discuss a discount. Please contact Hannah Grace-Williams on email info@chandospublishing.com or telephone number +44 (0) 1865 884447.

Weblogs and Libraries

LAUREL A. CLYDE

Chandos Publishing

Oxford · England · New Hampshire · USA

Chandos Publishing (Oxford) Limited
Chandos House
5 & 6 Steadys Lane
Stanton Harcourt
Oxford OX29 5RL
UK
Tel: +44 (0) 1865 884447 Fax: +44 (0) 1865 884448
Email: info@chandospublishing.com
www.chandospublishing.com

Chandos Publishing USA
3 Front Street, Suite 331
PO Box 338
Rollinsford, NH 03869
USA
Tel: 603 749 9171 Fax: 603 749 6155
Email: BizBks@aol.com

First published in Great Britain in 2004

ISBN:
1 84334 085 2 (paperback)
1 84334 096 8 (hardback)

© Laurel A. Clyde, 2004

British Library Cataloguing-in-Publication Data.
A catalogue record for this book is available from the British Library.

Printed in the UK and USA.

Contents

Acknowledgements

The following people and organisations gave permission for pictures of their weblogs or websites to be reproduced in this book; their cooperation is acknowledged with thanks:

- The ComLib Team, students in the 'Computers and Libraries' course at the University of Iceland in the spring of 2002, for the *ComLib* weblog;

- Salam Pax, for *Where is Raed?*, the weblog of the 'Baghdad Blogger';

- Sheila Webber, Department of Information Studies, University of Sheffield, United Kingdom, for the *Information Literacy Weblog*;

- Glenn Reynolds, for the *InstaPundit* weblog;

- The Daypop search engine;

- Steven M. Cohen, for the *Library Stuff* weblog;

- Anna Lewis, for *The Education Librarian* weblog;

- Rachel Peacock, Reference and Information Manager, Cultural Development, Gateshead Council, United Kingdom, for the Gateshead Public Library weblog;

- Lynn Dennis, Automation Coordinator/Technical Services Department Head, and Amy Cawley, Youth Services Department Head, Roselle Public Library, Illinois, USA, for the *Blogger Book Club* weblog.

Thanks to Sigurbjörg, Ösp and Sigríður for the two weeks before Icelandair flight FI 450 took off from Keflavík International Airport on 4 March 2004.

Anne Clyde
Durham, England
March 2004

List of figures

List of tables

Introduction

Weblogs, blogs, blogging, bloggers ... New additions to our vocabulary, representing new activities, new ways of communicating, new sources of information.

Weblogs (or just 'blogs') are a relatively new aspect of the World Wide Web, dating from around 1998 (though a few websites resembling today's weblogs were available earlier). The growth in the number of weblogs, and their impact, has been rapid. Futurist and professional 'trend spotter' Marion Salzman pointed to 2003 as the year when blogging really 'took hold'.[1] It was the year when the Baghdad blogger Salam Pax[2] and other 'warbloggers' provided an alternative to the mainstream media reporting of the invasion of Iraq and then found themselves a place in the mainstream media, with their weblog reports being covered by newspapers such as *The New York Times*, the *Los Angeles Times* and the *Guardian* (United Kingdom), and by networks such as the BBC, CNN and Voice of America. It was also a year in which 'people have made scores of new friends, gotten job offerings, and started companies' through their weblogs, says blogger Diego Dorval.[3] Estimates of the number of weblogs in existence at that stage ranged from fewer than two million to more than four million.

If 2003 was the year in which blogging took hold, 2004 was predicted to be the year when it would become trendy, according to *TheBlogSite* (in December 2003).[4] It was also predicted that in 2004 we would see more marketing via weblogs, as well as new applications for weblogs. However, *TheBlogSite* was curiously unspecific about what those applications might be – it seems that in the 'blogsphere', few people have the courage to make predictions, even for one year ahead.

The reaction to the growth of the weblog phenomenon has been mixed. On the one hand, it seems that 'there's now even more vapid content on the Web'[5] than before weblogs came along. This is certainly true in relation to many personal weblogs, which may report the blogger's day-to-day activities in mind-numbing detail. The things these 'bloggers seem to have in common is that they have a lot of time on their hands and an exhibitionist streak',[6] says Geoff Nunberg. An exchange student in Sydney, Australia, provides a record on his blog of everything he ate or drank (forget the school work); a Seattle couple write about walking the dog and going to the supermarket; a teenage girl agonises over which of two invitations she should accept for Saturday night; a bank clerk records daily confrontations with 'the boss'. On the other hand, some personal weblogs, particularly those that are thoughtful, interesting and well written, attract an ongoing readership in much the same way as paper-based 'zines (home-produced personal magazines) did in the 1980s and 1990s.

Taking the positive view, Peter Rojas has described weblogs as 'the hottest thing to happen to the web in years'. Considering that the World Wide Web only entered its teens a few years ago, this could be interpreted as a litle over-enthusiastic. However, Rojas does draw attention to the strengths of weblogs. He says, 'a weblogger surveys the vast world of the web and carefully arranges what's out there, presenting it in a new form ... A weblog functions like a filter for the web, a handpicked selection of what's worth checking out'.[7] Clearly this is not true of all weblogs, since some simply chronicle the day-to-day activities or present the opinions of the blogger.

While some personal weblogs contain little in the way of useful information, there are others that cover current developments in a particular subject field. Many experts or committed hobbyists who have created weblogs have seen those weblogs accepted as important sources of information on their topic. Library and information science is a case in point – weblogs like *LISNews*[8] and *Library Stuff*[9] discuss current professional news and issues long before printed newsletters and journals pick up on them.

Nevertheless, as the warbloggers showed, weblogs and print media have become, if not necessarily mutually dependent, then at least allies. Newspapers and news organisations use weblogs as information sources. Weblogs created by major newspapers, professional associations, government agencies and other organisations provide current information and comment, usually but not always as a way of updating information that they provide in print form. The *Guardian*, for example, one of Britain's most important newspapers, also has weblogs (established in November 2001) that cover general news and news about developments in technology. In fact, the *Guardian* has encouraged the development of quality weblogs in the United Kingdom by regular reporting on them and through its 'Best British Weblog' competition in 2003.

Journalism, like library and information science, is a field in which weblogs have made a significant impact. Indeed, weblogs have been hailed as 'creating a revolution in journalism ... [they are] the ultimate in free speech where you can speak your mind and have an outlet to share your thoughts and interests without the confines of traditional publishing ...'[10] Others claim that weblogs are not necessarily journalism at all, nor should they be promoted as such. Weblogs provide unedited statements of opinion and an outlet for alternative points of view and as such can have value, says a contributor to the *Kuro5hin*[11] weblog, but the same contributor hopes that 'few people engaged with the world enough to seek out these kinds of alternative voices are giving them the sort of credibility' that is usually accorded to the major newspapers.[12] 'Blogging has succeeded because it has made it possible for a solo web journalist to create and distribute his [*sic*] research, reporting, and written opinions'; on the other hand, 'it's now feasible for someone who is only mildly computer literate to create his [*sic*] own professional-looking regularly updated web site'.[13]

Just as weblogs have their connections to mainstream journalism, so they also have connections to the intimate reporting of reality television, to 'journaling' and the self-help ideas embodied in the personal story movement, and even to the duplicated Christmas letters that arrive from friends and family each year. Phil Gyford has created a weblog[14] for that greatest of diarists, Samuel Pepys, who for nearly ten years from 1660 wrote about his daily experiences, his amorous adventures and the events of the time.[15] Meanwhile, hundreds of thousands of present-day Pepys imitators are recording their annual holidays or the first year of life with their new baby or their progress through library school. When one of these weblogs incorporates photographs (perhaps taken with a digital camera), the visitor to the weblog sees the view from the Sydney Harbour Bridge, or Mum, Dad and very new baby posed on the steps of the hospital. When one of these weblogs incorporates a feed from a webcam (usually a video camera linked to the Internet) then the visitor (if logged on at the right time) sees the blogger getting ready for a date or baby's first faltering attempts to crawl. Many of these weblogs are probably more important for their creators than they are for any 'reading public'; the act of creating the blog is often the whole point.

Like the Internet as a whole, the world of blogging is not without its problems. A lot of weblogs allow, indeed encourage, readers to post comments. While interactive features can create a sense of community among bloggers and their readers, these features may also leave the weblog open to spamming from people who post the same message to thousands of weblogs.[16] Another negative aspect is the emergence of sex blogging. Just as a considerable portion of the World Wide Web is devoted to sex sites, so sex blogs (of various kinds) seem to account for a considerable proportion of weblogs. Porn blogs have also appeared on the scene. People who are exploring weblogs need to exercise the same care and caution that they would exercise in exploring the wider Web.

In other words, weblogs have their strengths and their limitations. There are things that weblogs do well, and there are applications for which weblogs are probably inappropriate. With Internet search engines like Google now including weblog posts in their search results, ordinary Internet users (as well as members of the blogging community) need some knowledge of the strengths and limitations of weblogs if they are to evaluate their search results. In order to assess the value of any information contained in a weblog, the reader also needs some knowledge of how weblogs are created. The same is true for the reader who is attempting to assess the literary or creative value of weblog content. Libraries are involved in information provision and in promoting and making available creative work, and so a knowledge of weblogs is important for librarians.

German weblog expert Martin Roell recommends weblogs as a means of improving business communication.

He suggests applications for weblogs in e-business, in knowledge management and for communciation within the business. In the latter application, a weblog based on the company's intranet, rather than a public weblog, might be appropriate.[17] In June 2003, a Weblog Business Conference and Expo held in Boston, Massachusetts, featured, among other topics, 'The New Communication Channel of Blogging' and 'The Success of Knowledge Blogs'. If weblogs can work in the business setting as a tool for communication among staff and with clients, then why not in libraries?

Are weblogs and libraries a natural combination? Many things suggest that they are. Weblogs are becoming more and more important as sources of information on a range of topics and as repositories of ideas and community experience. Weblogs are also being promoted as tools for delivering information to those who need it, and some companies and other organisations are investigating the use of weblogs as marketing tools. 'Libraries are in a perfect position to be at the "coal face" of this web activity', says Michelle Alcock in the Australian professional newsletter *Quill*.[18]

This book discusses the topic 'weblogs and libraries' from two main perspectives: weblogs as sources of information for libraries and librarians; and weblogs as tools that libraries can use to promote their services or to provide a means of communication with their clients. It begins with an overview of the whole weblog and blogging phenomenon and traces its development over the past five or six years. The many different kinds of weblogs (including personal weblogs, cooperative or community weblogs, and moblogs) are described, with examples. The problems associated with finding useful weblogs are addressed through a discussion of weblog directories, specialist search engines and other finding tools. One chapter, based on a research project carried out late in 2003, provides an overview of the 'state of the art' of library weblogs (that is, weblogs created by libraries). Other chapters are devoted to the options available for creating a weblog, and strategies for managing the library's own weblog.

Disclaimer

While sources of information about hardware, software and weblogs have been checked carefully, the Internet is a rapidly changing environment. Readers are advised to seek current information about products or weblogs, and URLs have been provided to assist. Neither the author nor the publisher can accept responsibility for information on weblogs or websites.

References

1. Marion Salzman, 'For a Happy New Year, Keep on Bonding', *Sunday Times* 28 Dec. 2003: News Review 5.
2. Salam Pax, *Salam Pax: The Clandestine Diary of an Ordinary Iraqi* (New York: Grove Press, 2003).
3. Diego Dorval, 'An Introduction to Weblogs', *d2r* [weblog] 31 Oct. 2003, online (available at *http://www.dynamicobjects .com/d2r/archives/002399.html* accessed 11 Nov. 2003).
4. 'Blogging Will Be Trendy in 2004', *TheBlogSite.com* 16 Dec. 2003, online (available at *http://www.theblogsite.com/12 .html* accessed 31 Jan. 2004).
5. Tim Archer, 'Wag Your Blog', *Trade Queer Things*, online (available at *http://www.tradequeerthings.com/online.html* accessed 16 Mar. 2002).

6. Geoff Nunberg, 'I Have Seen the Future, and It Blogs', Oct. 2001, online (available at *http://www-csli.stanford.edu/ ~nunberg/blog.html* accessed 16 Apr. 2002).

7. Peter Rojas, 'Second Sight', *Guardian Unlimited Online* [weblog] 1 May 2003, online (available at *http://www .guardian.co.uk/online/story/0,3605,946510,00.html* accessed 6 May 2003).

8. *http://lisnews.com/*

9. *http://www.librarystuff.net/*

10. Nigel Horrocks, 'Fifteen Minutes of Fame', *Australian NetGuide* Sep. 2003: 22.

11. *http://www.kuro5hin.org/*

12. 'Weblogs as Journalism', *Kuro5hin: Technology and Culture From the Trenches* [weblog] 11 Oct. 2001, online (available at *http://www.kuro5hin.org/story/2001/10/11/232538/32* accessed 16 Mar. 2002).

13. 'Weblogs – Blogging: An Economist's View', *Library Stuff* [weblog] 10 Apr. 2002, online (available at *http://www .librarystuff.net/* accessed 12 Apr. 2002).

14. *http://www.pepysdiary.com/*

15. 'Why I Turned Pepys' Diary Into a Weblog', *BBC News* 2 Jan. 2003, online (available at *http://news.bbc.co.uk/2/hi/uk_ news/2621581.stm* accessed 2 Jan. 2003).

16. Bill Thompson, 'How Spammers Are Targeting Blogs', *BBC News* 24 Oct. 2003, online (available at *http://news.bbc.co .uk/I/hi/technology/3210623.stm* accessed 1 Feb. 2004).

17. Martin Roell, quoted in 'Weblogs Can Improve Business?', *newsfox.digest* [online service] 26 May 2003, online (available at *http://www.pressetext.com/pte.mc?pte=030526047* accessed 26 May 2003). See also *http://www.roell.net/*

18. Michelle Alcock, 'Blogs – What Are They and How Do We Use Them?', *Quill* 103.8 (2003). Online (available at *http:// www.alia.org.au/members-only/groups/quill/issues/203.8/ blogs.html* accessed 8 Oct. 2003).

About the author

Dr L. Anne Clyde is Professor in the Faculty of Social Science at the University of Iceland. An Australian citizen, she has degrees from the University of Sydney and the James Cook University of North Queensland and is an Associate of the Australian Library and Information Association. She is also a Fellow of CILIP in the United Kingdom and a Member of the Australian College of Educators.

Having held a number of library and academic positions in Australia, Dr Clyde accepted a short-term appointment as a visiting faculty member at the University of Iceland for a year, then in 1991 moved to the University of British Columbia in Canada as Associate Professor with responsibility for Teacher Librarianship programmes. After two years there, she returned to Iceland to her present position.

Her teaching responsibilities within the library and information science programme at the University of Iceland are in the general area of information technology and its use. She is also an Internet trainer and has conducted Internet courses through the Division of Continuing Education at the University of Iceland for lawyers, business people, librarians, journalists, nurses and others; she also conducts Internet courses in other countries.

Her current research interests relate to the use of the Internet and online information services in a range of settings. She is working on a number of projects related to the Internet, including the development of quality indicators for school library websites. She has also carried out research and/or consultancies for a number of organisations and institutions, including the European Commission. In addition, she undertakes research and development projects through her own consultancy, Netweaver.

Dr Clyde has published extensively in the field. She has written ten books and her articles have appeared in both national and international journals. She also writes a regular column on 'InfoTech' for the North American journal *Teacher Librarian*.

Dr Clyde has served for ten years as Webmaster for the International Association of School Librarianship; the website, called School Libraries Online, can be found at *http://www.iasl-slo.org/*. She also maintains a teaching page about weblogs at *http://www.hi.is/~anne/weblogs.html*.

The author may be contacted as follows:

Dr L. Anne Clyde, Professor
Faculty of Social Science
The University of Iceland
101 Reykjavik
Iceland

E-mail: *anne@hi.is*
Website: *http://www.hi.is/~anne/*

An overview of the weblog and blogging phenomenon

Depending on your point of view, weblogs are either one of the most important Internet developments of recent years or one of the silliest; although they have a lot of advocates, they also have a lot of detractors. On the one hand, it is claimed that weblogs are empowering because 'anyone' (or any group of people) can create a weblog to share their thoughts and ideas with the world – a claim which is certainly not true, since 'anyone' would need access to the Internet and some information handling skills. On the other hand, it is also claimed that weblogs 'are pointless, self-indulgent or interesting only to a small circle of people'[1] and that they add considerably to the already large amount of dubious content on the Web, making it harder to find reliable or useful material. There is a sense in which both perspectives are valid: there are some well-maintained, high-quality weblogs that provide a valuable service, but there are also many weblogs that serve no apparent purpose apart from providing the owner with an online public space. Sheer numbers, though, suggest that weblogs cannot be ignored.

What are weblogs?

Canadian weblog expert Peter Scott[2] has developed a widely accepted definition of a 'blog' or 'weblog': it is, he says, 'a Web page containing brief, chronologically arranged items of information'. At this point, though, any agreement about weblogs ends. Some commentators insist that weblogs are 'personal websites, usually maintained by an individual, constantly updated with new information, personal experiences, analysis, hyperlinks and commentary'.[3] However, not all weblogs are personal websites: institutions (including libraries, professional associations and companies) have created what they themselves describe as weblogs. Further, not all personal (or other) weblogs contain external links to other Internet resources; weblogs that exist primarily to 'publish' an individual's creative writing are a case in point. For Theresa Ross Embrey, weblogs are 'a cross between a diary, a web site, and an online community'.[4] However, not all weblogs provide interactive facilities through which readers might become part of a virtual community based on the weblog. Some commentators insist that a weblog has to be created with special-purpose weblog software (such as Blogger or Radio UserLand, of which more in Chapter 6). However, many of the sites created without such weblog software are to all intents and purposes indistinguishable from weblogs – and many of them appear in the directories of weblogs such as the comprehensive list at Yahoo![5]

For a number of reasons, trying to define a weblog may be an exercise in futility. First, the weblog scene is changing all the time, as new developments in technology make it possible for bloggers to do new things. Secondly, regardless of any definitions of blogging, bloggers will continue to test the boundaries of what is possible – after all, blogging came into existence in part as a response to the perceived restrictions of the existing media. Thirdly, it is the most common features of weblogs and similar sites that are important for readers, regardless of definitions. These common features, such as chronological arrangement of items (with the most recent first), frequency of updating, provision of links to Internet sources and the incorporation of comments from readers, help to make weblogs appealing, but also make it difficult for Internet users to locate weblogs and to evaluate the information in them.

A weblog can take any one of a number of forms. It might be a personal journal or diary, or the public diary of a political leader, or the journal of an expedition, or the record of a family holiday. It could be a news service (or provide summaries of and links to current news items on a topic). It could be a collection of links to other websites, perhaps with annotations or commentary. It could be a series of book reviews, reports of activity on a project, a photographic record of life with a new puppy or the random thoughts of an egomaniac. The potential is almost endless. Professional photographers create weblogs to show off their photographs (as do the proud parents of new babies). Musicians create weblogs with embedded sound files of their work. Elementary school classes have created weblogs to record their work on group projects; libraries have created weblogs to provide information to their users; newspapers have weblogs to update stories in the printed edition of the paper. Some weblogs exist to provide one point of view (that of the blogger); others exist to bring together a range of viewpoints on a topic.

Browsing through some of the directories of weblogs (see Chapter 3) suggests that the majority of weblogs are created as single-person efforts. Some professional weblogs are created by experts in their subject field, who monitor news services and other online sources of information and summarise and comment on that news for their readers; they also provide links to the original online source. At the other end of the scale, we find a range of personal weblogs whose titles, such as *Mere Trivia* or *A Whole Lotta Nothin'*, might be said to reflect their content. Other weblogs are created as cooperative or group projects. An example of a cooperative weblog is the *Illinois Library Association's ILA RTSF Technology Users Group Web Logger – The Forum*,[6] which aims to provide community web space for the group.

Many claims have been made for the usefulness of weblogs. At their best, they can 'help readers cope with an information avalanche', says Andy Wang,[7] by highlighting and summarising useful material. Rebecca Blood[8] (creator of the *Rebecca's Pocket* weblog[9]) suggests that they can also 'contextualize' an article by listing it among related articles from different sources, so that 'each article, considered in the light of the other, may take on additional meaning'. Weblogs created in response to a major event may provide a range of perspectives that would be missed by the conventional media: the weblogs that appeared immediately after the 9/11 World Trade Center attacks or the 'warblogs' that emerged after the invasion of Iraq are examples. Weblogs may bring to the attention of the reader material that would otherwise have been missed because the reader does not normally monitor all sources of information on a topic. On the other hand, weblogs are part of the 'information avalanche', and perhaps part of the problem.

The history of weblogs

Weblogs, of the kind with which we are familiar today, are a relatively recent Internet phenomenon dating from the late 1990s. For many people, the emergence of the Blogger weblog development software (made available by Pyra Labs in 1999) defined the beginnings of 'blogging', though the Pitas software was available several months before Blogger. With its slogan of 'push-button publishing for the people',[10] Blogger 'changed the face of the web', said Neil McIntosh[11] in the British newspaper the *Guardian*. While this is probably considerably overstating the case, the Blogger home page's promise of 'instant communication power by letting you post your thoughts to the web whenever the urge strikes' was something that many found attractive. For the people who access the weblogs (as distinct from the bloggers who create them), part of the appeal lies in the fact that anyone who can use a web browser can read a weblog – no special software is needed and there are no new skills to be learned.

Kevin Werbach, writing in 2001, noted that while 'personal homepages and online diaries have been around since the early days of the web', the 'earliest sites to call themselves weblogs began around 1997'.[12] Other writers see weblogs as being a little older. 'The first weblogs appeared in the early 1990s, and were collections of links and information the authors found worthy of compiling or catagorizing as they journeyed around the World Wide Web'.[13] On the other hand, the online diaries such as Justin Hall's *Links From the Underground* (1994) that were begun around the same time have been identified by Dylan Tweney[14] as the 'ancestors' of the weblog. To a certain extent, each writer's understanding of the history of blogging is dependent upon their own definition of a weblog. All seem to agree that regardless of when and how weblogs really began, blogging became more accessible and popular when free software for creating weblogs appeared on the scene in 1999.

Certainly, in the second half of that year, the number of weblogs had grown sufficiently for a directory to be considered useful, and Brigitte Eaton developed the *Eatonweb Portal* as a list of every 'site consisting of dated entries' that she could find.[15] By the end of January 2002, *Wired* magazine reported a new record: in that month alone, some 41,000 people created new weblogs using Blogger's free service[16] – and Blogger was only one of the weblog maintenance tools by then available. Weblog numbers continued to increase, though it had also become clear that many weblogs ceased to be updated after the blogger's first flush of enthusiasm passed.

Estimates of the number of publicly available weblogs in existence in 2003 ranged from 1.5 million[17] to 4.12 million.[18] In part, the differences among the various estimates can be accounted for by the different ways in which different commentators define weblogs. In addition, a survey of weblogs, carried out by Perseus Development Corporation in late 2003, confirmed the increasing number of abandoned weblogs (which nevertheless show up in search engine results). Of the weblogs in the Perseus sample, 66 per cent had not been updated in the previous two months and most of these had 'been either permanently or temporarily abandoned'.[19] On the other hand, Maciej Ceglowski, who analysed a larger sample of weblogs earlier in the year, found that 65 per cent *had* been updated within the previous eight weeks and 60 per cent had been updated within the previous three weeks.[20] This presents a rather different picture of the 'blogsphere'. Either way, it leaves a large number of weblogs that are being maintained on an ongoing basis. Further, that number is increasing rapidly.

There is further evidence of rapid development of blogging from 1998–99 onwards in the print newspapers.

A search for articles that mention weblogs or blogs or blogging or bloggers in four newspaper databases on the DIALOG commercial online information service is summarised in Table 1.1. Searches of the *New York Times* database, the *Boston Globe* database, the Canadian Newspapers Database, and *The Times* and *Sunday Times* (London) database showed no use of any of these terms before 1998, and only the Canadian Newspapers Database had articles in which the terms were used before 1999. For all four databases, there was a substantial increase in the use of these terms from 2001 to 2002, and another substantial increase from 2002 to 2003. The number of articles in which these terms were used was smallest in *The Times* and *Sunday Times*. However, these newspapers sometimes used the term 'online diary' rather than 'weblog' or 'blog', and if articles that use this term are factored in, then *The Times* and *Sunday Times* results follow the same pattern as for the other newspapers. By 2003, blogging was definitely newsworthy; articles about blogging were appearing at least twice a week in *The New York Times*, for example.

Table 1.1 Articles that mention weblogs or blogging: newspapers in the USA, the UK and Canada

Year	New York Times (USA)	Boston Globe (USA)	Canadian Newspaper Database	The Times (UK)
1998	–	–	3	–
1999	–	–	3	2
2000	–	1	7	3
2001	6	4	21	4
2002	47	16	36	19
2003	128	63	195	27

Who creates weblogs?

The quick answer to the question, 'Who creates weblogs?' is often 'Almost anybody'. However, bloggers do need to have ready access to the Internet, which eliminates a large proportion of the world's population. They also need some computer skills and some Internet search skills. Furthermore, even though products like Blogger[21] and Radio Userland[22] promised instant communication power by enabling users to post their thoughts and ideas to the Web whenever they wanted, the process was not quite as simple as the home pages of these products suggested. In fact, though specialist weblog software considerably simplified the process of web page creation, the documentation and procedures still assume at least a basic level of knowledge of FTP (File Transfer Protocol), website structures and technical terms. For those who want to go beyond the basic weblog templates, some knowledge of HTML is necessary. However, hundreds of thousands, if not millions, of people have used these products successfully to create weblogs.

Personal websites created by individuals fall into two main categories: personal diaries and professional or information sites. The best of the former are 'those spearheaded by strong personalities', says John M. Grohol, 'dynamic individuals who have something to say',[23] though some are driven simply by the power of good writing. Sometimes it is a combination of factors: Meg Hourihan, for example, who owns the *Megnut*[24] blog, not only writes beautifully but is also known in the blogging community as one of the people behind the Pyra group who developed the Blogger software. The best of the professional or information blogs are those created by experts in their field who are prepared to share that expertise with others through a weblog. Steven Bell cautions, though, that 'it is the very rare person who can keep coming up with worthy thoughts and observations on a daily basis',[25] and this comment is borne out in the professional weblogs, regardless of topic. Most fields now have such experts; the field of library and information science is particularly fortunate in that a number of practitioners and academics have created professional weblogs, though not all are of equal value. Some of the weblogs in the field of library and information science will be discussed in Chapter 4.

Why do people blog? Many reasons have been suggested and the motivating factors are almost certainly as varied as the people who blog. In terms of diary-type blogs, John C. Dvorak, columnist with *PC Magazine*, suggests, somewhat disparagingly, that their creators are looking for ego gratification, or a way to demonstrate their individuality, or to vent their frustration with day-to-day life, or just because of a human need to share. Some bloggers are simply 'wannabe writers',[26] using a weblog as a way to get started. In terms of professional weblogs, Marylaine Block, writing in *Library Journal*, suggests that the reasons for blogging include community service, sharing expertise, providing an alternative to the trade magazines, creating opportunities for cooperation or just having fun. She also acknowledges that some people might be in it to make money or for career advantage.[27]

However, it is not just individuals or groups of individuals who blog. Weblogs are also created by organisations and institutions of various kinds, including companies, professional associations, universities and colleges, libraries, clubs ... The purposes that these weblogs are designed to serve include publicity and promotion, sharing of information or knowledge management within an organisation, communicating with clients or the local community, influencing public opinion, testing products or ideas, or creating opportunities for assessing public opinion.

Types of weblogs

Weblogs can be categorised in a number of different ways – on the basis of the content, the format or features, the purpose or aim of the weblog, the way the weblog was created, the way in the weblog is made available, and the characteristics of the blogger or bloggers who maintain the weblog, among other things.

Nigel Horrocks, writing in *Australian NetGuide* in September 2003,[28] listed five different types of weblog on the basis of their content and purpose. The first was the weblog based on the 'daily thoughts' of the blogger; this usually takes the form of short diary entries, sometimes with photographs. His second type of weblog consists of 'interesting stuff' the blogger has found online, almost always with links and usually with commentary. The third type consists of 'thought-provoking comment' – opinions about news and current events or about just one issue, with the aim of getting a reaction and perhaps creating change. The fourth type, family blogs, are usually a group effort and may or may not be accessible to the general public. Finally, 'information blogs' are exactly what the name suggests – a way for people or organisations to share information of various kinds. Horrocks notes than many weblogs could be listed in more than one of these categories.

Like Horrocks, Cindy Curling categorises weblogs on the basis of their content or purpose, though her categories are different. She identified four useful 'blog flavors' in an article for *LLRX.com* (a legal information website) in 2001: 'the researcher's list of annotated resources, the extremely succinct pointer site, the more personal annotated journal, and the personal diary'.[29] She also alluded in the article to 'me' weblogs which, while sometimes interesting, are not the kind of weblog that would normally be used at work or for professional purposes.

Another way of understanding weblogs is by the way in which they are made available. Public weblogs are available on the Internet for anyone to read. They may be included in the results of searches on public search engines such as Google, and they may be listed in directories of weblogs. Private weblogs, on the other hand, are either available on the Internet but with access restricted in some way (for example by password) or are available only on an intranet within an organisation such as a company or a university or a school. Public weblogs and private weblogs are usually created and maintained in much the same way. Weblogs in both groups may fall into any of the content or purpose categories listed by Horrocks or Curling, or they may take other forms.

Many weblogs are designed for one-way communication – from the blogger to the reader. Others, however, are interactive, providing facilities for two-way communication. Interactivity allows readers to play a role in the development of the weblog, sometimes creating a virtual community around the weblog. Social network theory[30] helps to explain why weblogs have such a large social influence, given the relatively small number of bloggers in relation to the total population of our planet. The ties among people who are not closely related have been shown to be important for spreading new ideas and for bringing people together for action.[31] At its simplest level, interactivity is based on enabling readers to comment on the 'posts' of the weblog 'owner' and on the comments of other readers, with all comments being available on the weblog.

A step up from this is the facility for readers to originate discussion through posts to the weblog rather than just responding to the posts of the weblog owner. Some weblogs allow readers to contribute photographs or sound files as well as text. Other places on the Internet provide inter-activity – for example, online message boards, USENET newsgroups, and listservs or e-mail groups. However, the process may be simpler or more intuitive for readers through a weblog.

Some of the most interesting weblogs are created as coop-erative or group projects rather than as the efforts of individual bloggers. In this case, the weblog owner can give 'posting rights' to other people, and their posts may or may not (depending on the 'rights' assigned by the owner) be reviewed before they are 'published' to the weblog page. Some weblogs are set up in such a way that only the owner or the owner and certain other people have posting rights, but anyone else can add comments to the posts. An example of a cooperative weblog is *ComLib*, created in the first half of 2002 by students in the 'Computers and Libraries' course at the University of Iceland.[32] *ComLib* carried news about websites related to the use of information technology in libraries. All of the students in the class posted messages to the weblog, but it was not set up to allow comments from people outside the ComLib Team. The *EdBlogger Praxis* weblog[33] records a number of examples of collaborative weblogs in elementary and secondary schools, serving a variety of instructional purposes. Within a business, a private weblog on an intranet may be one tool in a know-ledge management strategy; in a professional association, a weblog (whether public or private) might be used as a 'platform' for developing a group project.

Mobile phones that take photographs and digital cameras with Internet capabilities have led to the development of

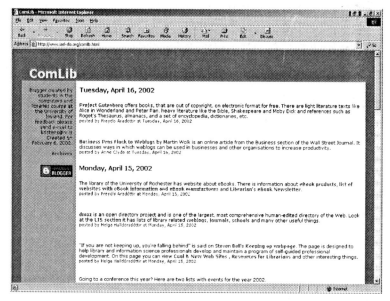

Figure 1.1 *ComLib*, a weblog created by students in the 'Computers and Libraries' course in the Library and Information Science Department at the University of Iceland, Spring Semester 2002

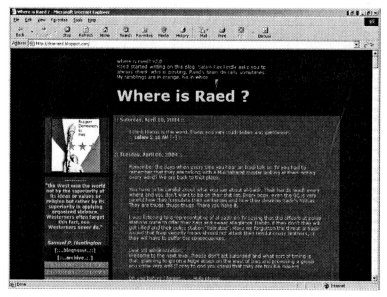

Figure 1.2 *Where is Raed?*, the weblog of the 'Baghdad Blogger', Salam Pax

'photoblogs'. 'Some photoblogs focus only on photography, while others have photos in addition to other content. All photoblogs, however, consider photos to be an important part of their chronological blogging structure', says the FAQ (frequently asked questions) document on the *Photoblogs.org* website.[34] But photoblogs are not the only new development in blogging. The phenomenon of 'moblogging' (blogging from a mobile device such as a mobile phone or a handheld computer), which has become more and more popular over the past two years, will be discussed below.

Common features of weblogs

Some of the basic features of weblogs were mentioned above, including the chronological arrangement of items (with the most recent first), frequency of updating, provision of links to Internet sources and the incorporation of comments from readers. Some weblogs have other useful features – for example, links to similar weblogs, or links to the most important Internet resources in the field of coverage of the weblog, or a way to make contact with other people who read the weblog, or access to software and services. Other common features of quality weblogs include the following:

- *Weblog archives*. The posts to the weblog are preserved on the site after they have moved off the current page. The archives are usually available for browsing by date of posting (month and year); on some weblogs, the archives can be searched by keyword as well.

- *Weblog search engine*. The provision of a search facility allows readers to search for posts that are no longer on the current page. While most weblog search engines provide for keyword searching by topic, some also provide for searching by the name of the person who posts (where a weblog allows readers to post comments).

- *Permalinks – 'permanent links'*. These are a way to give a unique URL to each post on a weblog so that when the post is transferred to the weblog archive it can still be accessed using the same URL that it had when it appeared at the top of the 'current page' of the weblog on the day it was written. Using permalinks tends to result in long URLs (particularly if there are a lot of posts to the weblog). Nevertheless, if the URL of any post is saved, it should continue to work for the reader.

- *Webcam*. A still or movie camera linked to the Internet can be used to provide a continuous 'feed' of images to a weblog. A webcam can be used to show an event in progress, to broadcast a conference presentation, to give an indication of what is happening in a classroom, to allow readers to watch animals in a zoo ...

- *Opinion polls*. Some weblogs continually poll their readers on issues relevant to the subject coverage of the weblog (with a running total available on the weblog), giving a sense of interactivity and also providing an indication of current opinion.

New features are being added to weblogs all the time, so that weblogs in general are becoming more sophisticated. However, this has happened mostly without the need for people who access the weblogs to download additional software or even add plugins to their web browser. Weblogs continue to be easy to read; further, they have retained a quality that was one of the sources of their early appeal – users do not need to acquire new skills in order to access them.

Moblogging

A relatively new form of blogging activity is 'moblogging' or 'mblogging' or 'phone blogging', to create a 'moblog'. As indicated above, this is blogging from a mobile phone or handheld. Moblogging might involve updating a 'traditional' weblog via SMS or e-mail from a phone or handheld, or adding photographs or sound to a 'traditional' weblog from a camera phone. Or it might involve the creation of a moblog using specialist moblog software and maintaining it only by mobile. For people who have a camera phone with wireless access to the World Wide Web, there are now specialist sites that allow them to create a digital journal and update it by phone.[35] While many moblogs are simply a record of a holiday or a school project, others present news as it happens, sometimes from a perspective that is different from that which appears in newspapers or on the television. 'The trend is set to transform an already successful web medium into something new, at-hand, and suited to our increasingly mobile lifestyles', says Amy Cowen.[36] Bloggers can blog from the street, the airport, the conference room or from the middle of an event. University students are blogging from the lecture theatre (a new way of taking lecture notes); library users are blogging from the stacks. This is 'anytime, anywhere', 24/7 blogging.

RSS and its use in weblogs

Weblogs and RSS have become closely interlinked. RSS is an attempt to address the problem of 'too much information on the Internet', to provide an effective way for serious Web users to keep track of new information in their own specialist fields. RSS has also become a tool that bloggers can use to distribute the content of their weblog more widely to people who may never visit the weblog. RSS stands for either 'Rich Site Summary' or 'Real Simple Syndication' or 'RDF Site Summary' (referring to the Resource Description Framework), depending on the commentator, the version of RSS and the software used. Different software developers have used RSS in different ways as a term, and this is one of the reasons that so many people find it so difficult to understand it.

With RSS, users can have content from websites such as weblogs and news sites delivered to a 'news aggregator' or reader on their own computer – and have that content updated all the time. A news aggregator (such as Feedreader[37] or NewzCrawler[38] or Headline Reader[39]) is a piece of software (available via the Internet) that can be configured to receive these news feeds and to display them for reading. These news aggregators can receive feeds from sites (including weblogs) that have been set up with RSS feed capabilities (using XML, that is eXtensible Markup Language). This feed received by the news aggregator enables the user to get information whenever something changes on a nominated weblog or news service or other website with an RSS feed. The user can check all updates in the one place, removing the need to go to a large number of weblogs and other sites each day to collect information. Lists of RSS aggregators or readers are available from the *Lockergnome* website of Chris Pirillo[40] and from Peter Scott's website.[41] For those who do not wish to install an aggregator or reader on their own computer, some public aggregators are available for use on the web. One such is *Bloglines*,[42] a free service that enables people to collect the RSS feeds of the weblogs they want to read and to monitor updates. Meanwhile, some people have created publicly available pages (using an aggregator) to bring together RSS feeds in a particular field for the benefit of other readers; these services are sometimes known as 'rollups' (from the name of a software package). An example of a rollup in the field of library and information science is *LISFeeds*;[43] it brings together current posts from those professional weblogs that provide an RSS feed so that they can be read on the one web page.

Increasingly, quality weblogs are being developed with RSS capabilities, just as news websites are, because the news aggregators are a way of bringing new readers to a website or distributing weblog content more widely. A few libraries are using RSS feeds on their weblogs or websites to provide users with information about new books in the library catalogue. What RSS makes possible is the delivery of timely information to the computer desktop of a user, without the user having to take any step other than the intial one of setting up and configuring a news aggregator.

The same kinds of claims are now being made for RSS that were made for weblogs themselves, and before them for web pages – that is, that RSS will change the face of publishing as we know it, and/or change the face of the Internet. For a number of reasons, this is unlikely. RSS is really a tool for distribution of web-based information, a form of syndication rather than a form of original publishing. What RSS does do is enable a reader to scan news stories and information from a wide variety of web-based sources without having to search. It is certainly having an effect on the way people access information on weblogs. There are already people who read material from weblogs regularly through an aggregator but who never see a weblog unless it has an RSS feed.

The development of services such as RSS highlight the continuing growth and impact of weblogs. Features such as archives, site search engines and RSS feeds have enabled them to move from hobbyist status to become serious information tools. The next chapter will discuss weblogs as sources of current information, with examples of quality weblogs from a number of fields. Chapter 3 will deal with finding weblogs, with an emphasis on finding information weblogs, while Chapter 4 will discuss weblogs in the library and information science environment.

References

1. Kevin Werbach, 'Triumph or the Weblogs', *Edventure* 18 Jun. 2001, online (available at *http://www.edventure.com/ conversation/article.cfm?Counter=7444662* accessed 16 March 2002).
2. Peter Scott, 'Blogging: Creating Instant Content for the Web', online (available at *http://library.usask.ca/~scottp/il2001/ definitions.html* accessed 15 Apr. 2002).
3. Maish Nichani and Venkat Rajamanickam, 'Grassroots KM Through Blogging', *Elearningpost* 14 May 2001, online (available at *http://www.elearningpost.com/features/archives/ 001009.asp* accessed 13 Dec. 2002).
4. Theresa Ross Embrey, 'You Blog, We Blog: A Guide to How Teacher-Librarians Can Use Weblogs to Build Communication and Research Skills', *Teacher Librarian*, 30.2 (2002): 7–9.
5. *http://dir.yahoo.com/Computers_and_Internet/Internet/ World_Wide_Web/Weblogs/*
6. It is unclear (March 2004) whether or not this site is still being maintained.
7. Andy Wang, 'Online Digest Helps Readers to Cope With Information Avalanche', *New York Times* 2 Aug. 1999, online (available at *http://www.nytimes.com/library/tech/99/ 08/biztech/articles/02link.html* accessed 15 Apr. 2002).
8. Rebecca Blood, 'Weblogs: A History and Perspective', *Rebecca's Pocket* [weblog] 7 Sep. 2000, online (available at

http://www.rebeccablood.net/essays/weblog_history.html accessed 15 Apr. 2002).

9. *http://www.rebeccablood.net/*

10. Biz Stone, 'Labs, Robots and Giant Floating Brains: The Amazingly True Story of Blogger!', *Webreview* 9 Mar. 2001, online (available at *http://www.webreview.com/2001/03_09/strategists/index02.shtml* accessed 15 Apr. 2002).

11. Neil McIntosh, 'A Tale of One Man and His Blog', *Guardian* 31 Jan. 2002, online (available at *http://www.guardian.co.uk/online/story/0,3605,641742,00.html* accessed 15 Apr. 2002).

12. Kevin Werbach, 'Triumph of the Weblogs', *Edventure* 18 Jun. 2001, online (available at *http://www.edventure.com/conversation/article.cfm?Counter=7444662* accessed 16 Mar. 2002).

13. Denise M. Howell, 'Law Meets Blog: Electronic Publishing Comes of Age', *LLRX.com* 1 May 2002, online (available at *http://www.llrx.com/features/lawblog.htm* accessed 4 May 2002).

14. Dylan Tweney, 'Weblogs Make the Web Work for You', *Business 2.0* 14 Feb. 2002, online (available at *http://www.business2.com/articles/web/0,1653,37974,FF.html* accessed 24 Mar. 2002).

15. *http://portal.eatonweb.com/*

16. Farhad Manjoo, 'Blah, Blah, Blah and Blog', *Wired* 18 Feb. 2002, online (available at *http://www.wired.com/news/culture/0,1284,50443,00.html* accessed 15 Mar. 2002).

17. Phil Wolff, 'The Blogcount Estimate: 2.4 to 2.9 Million Blogs', *Blogcount* [weblog] 23 Jun. 2003, online (available at *http://dijest.com/bc/* accessed 8 Sep. 2003).

18. Perseus Development Corporation, 'The Blogging Iceberg', *Resource Shelf* [weblog] 5 Oct. 2003, online (available at *http://www.resourceshelf.com/2003_10_01_resourceshelf_archive.html* accessed 10 Oct. 2003).

19. Perseus Development Corporation, 'The Blogging Iceberg', *Resource Shelf* [weblog] 5 Oct. 2003, online (available at *http://www.resourceshelf.com/2003_10_01_resourceshelf_archive.html* accessed 10 Oct. 2003).

20. Phil Wolff, 'Wandering Through the Weblog Cemetery', *Blogcount* [weblog] 27 Jul. 2003, online (available at *http://dijest.com/bc/* accessed 8 Sep. 2003).

21. *http://www.blogger.com/*

22. *http://www.userland.com/*

23. John M. Grohol, 'Psychology of Weblogs', *PsychCentral* Apr. 2001, online (available at *http://www.psychcentral.com/ blogs/* accessed 16 Mar. 2002).

24. *http://www.megnut.com/*

25. Steven Bell, in Walt Crawford, 'Weblogs and Libraries', *Cites & Insights* 3.11 (2003): 17–20.

26. John C. Dvorak, 'The Blog Phenomenon', *PC Magazine* 5 Feb. 2002, online (available at *http://www.pcmag.com/ article/0,2997,s%253D1493%2526a%253D21865,00.asp* accessed 16 Mar. 2002).

27. Marylaine Block, 'Communicating Off the Page', *Library Journal* 15 Sep. 2001, online (available at *http://www.libdex .com/marylaine.html* accessed 16 Mar. 2002).

28. Nigel Horrocks, '15 Minutes of Fame', *Australian NetGuide* Sep. 2003: 20–27.

29. Cindy Curling, 'Notes from the Technology Trenches: A Closer Look at Weblogs', *LLRX.com* 15 Oct. 2001, online (available at *http://www.llrx.com/columns/notes46.htm* accessed 16 Mar. 2002).

30. Mark Granovetter, 'The Strength of Weak Ties', *American Journal of Sociology* 78.6 (1093): 1360–1380.

31. James Moore, 'A Theoretical Note on Why Blogs Matter: The Strength of Weak Ties', *Jim Moore's Cybernetics, Politics, Emergence* [weblog] 1 Jan. 2004, online (available at *http:// blogs.law.harvard.edu/jim/2004/01/01#a398* accessed 2 Feb. 2004).

32. Laurel A. Clyde, 'Blogging Our Way Through a Course', *Personnel Training and Education* 20.1 (2003): 1–4.

33. *http://educational.blogs.com/edbloggerpraxis/*

34. *http://www.photoblogs.org/faq/*

35. 'Married to the Mob(log)?', *ABCNEWS.com* 29 Jul. 2003, online (available at *http://abcnews.go.com/sections/scitech/ FutureTech/moblogging030729.html* accessed 28 Aug. 2003).

36. Amy Cowen, 'Blogging Goes Mobile', *m-pulse magazine* 8 Sep. 2003, online (available at *http://www.cooltown.com/mpulse/0803-mblogging.asp* accessed 8 Sep. 2003).
37. *http://www.feedreader.com/*
38. *http://www.newzcrawler.com/*
39. *http://www.headlinereader.com/*
40. *http://rss.lockergnome.com/resources/*
41. *http://www.lights.com/weblogs/rss.html*
42. *http://www.bloglines.com/*
43. *http://www.librarystuff.net/rssfeeds/lisfeeds/*

2

Weblogs as sources of current information

Weblogs as sources of information

Belinda Weaver, in her 'Weaver's Web' column for the Australian Library and Information Association (ALIA) newsletter *InCite* in September 2003, said, 'The more I use web logs, the more I find the format perfect for current awareness'.[1] Though many personal weblogs are 'a waste of time', she says, the best 'contain useful postings' that help their readers to keep up to date. Indeed, as predicted by New Orleans lawyer Ernest Svenson (who as 'Ernie the Attorney' writes a well-known blog), many weblogs have emerged as authoritative sources of information in their fields.[2] Writing in the CILIP (Chartered Institute of Librarians and Information Professionals, United Kingdom) magazine *Update*, Hazel D'Aguiar answers the question of whether or not weblogs are useful to information professionals. She says:

> I have felt much more up to date with issues affecting libraries ... since starting to read blogs, and have enjoyed being part of a wider community of bloggers, and that is just by commenting ... blogs provide us with a beautifully simple method of developing a global community for the exchange of knowledge.[3]

The best information weblogs are authoritative sources of current information and opinion related to their topic. In the lists of weblogs below, we can see some that are created by well-known people in their field, for example the *Scholarly Electronic Publishing Weblog*[4] created by Charles W. Bailey Jr and the *Information Literacy Weblog*[5] created by Sheila Webber. Some of the other weblogs in the list are backed by a respected institution such as a major newspaper (for example, *Guardian Unlimited: The Weblog*[6] from the British newspaper the *Guardian*) or a university (for example, *JURIST: The Paper Chase*[7] from the University of Pittsburgh School of Law). Not only are many information weblogs actually created by subject experts (or at least by people with an abiding interest in a subject), but they often attract the participation of other experts through the 'comment' facility. Other weblogs in the list have gained respect for the quality of the writing, the value of the information or their unique point of view.

A major strength of weblogs is the ease with which they can be updated, whether from the desktop or by mobile phone. In the case of an information weblog, this should lead to more frequent updating. The typical weblog format, in which the most recent information appears first, highlights this aspect. Another strength of many information weblogs is their references to a range of opinions, as well as links to other sources of information and commentary. Further, since most information weblogs contain not only links embedded in the posts, but also links to other recommended weblogs in the subject area, a good weblog can lead to other useful resources. They can be used at the reference desk or in the provision of information services; they can also be the basis of professional reading and professional development activities.

There are, however, problems associated with using weblogs as sources of current information, not all of which affect every weblog. First, finding quality weblogs is not easy. At one level, 'the proliferation of blogging sites makes it especially difficult for consumers to know which bloggers they would find interesting'.[8] At another level, although weblog entries appear in the search results of the major search engines, there is no comprehensive listing of weblogs, nor is there a specialist search engine that covers the whole 'blogsphere'. This problem of locating weblogs will be addressed in more detail in Chapter 3. Secondly, it is not always easy to identify the person responsible for the weblog (the 'Baghdad Blogger'[9] is a famous example). Nor is it easy to identify the people who are responsible for comments posted to weblogs – and the greater the degree of interactivity (a feature that is usually viewed as something positive), the harder it is follow up on the sources of the comments. Thirdly, the pressure of maintaining an active weblog and the demands on the time of experts may mean that the content of a weblog may be uneven. Finally, there are at present no widely accepted criteria or procedures for evaluating the weblogs (or the inormation they contain), so that they can be used with confidence as sources of information.

Evaluating weblogs as sources of information

Evaluation serves different purposes. Some people are attempting to select the 'best weblogs', for example for listing in a directory. But just what does 'the best' mean? The most entertaining? The most reliable as a source of information? The most attractive in a visual sense? Some organisations are evaluating their own weblogs as part of the project development cycle within the organisation. Is the weblog serving the purpose for which it was designed? Has it achieved its goals? Bloggers evaluate other weblogs in order to make decisions about whether or not to link to them. Readers are making decisions about which weblogs to add to their list of 'Favorites' or which RSS feeds to add to their aggregator. Librarians have the additional responsibility of evaluating resources on behalf of other people, the users of the library or information service. To which weblogs will the library website link? Which RSS feeds will be added to the library's aggregator for the benefit of library users?

Selecting 'the best' weblogs, one of the forms of evaluation, becomes important in the context of awards. The annual Weblog Awards, known as 'The Bloggies', commenced in 2001.[10] These are publicly nominated and publicly chosen awards for creators of weblogs, weblog writers and other people associated with weblogs. There are a number of categories, including 'Something that helps you publish, make comments, anything that has to do with developing a weblog', 'Photoblogs and other weblogs that regularly feature photography', 'Weblogs about web design and development', plus the 'Weblog of the Year' award. However, there do not seem to be any stated criteria for these awards, or, indeed, any information on the Bloggies website about what 'the best' might mean in this context.

Some people rely on well-known sites to do their filtering (or evaluation) for them; these sites 'function almost as a magazine editor does',[11] searching out and linking to quality weblogs. One of these sites is *InstaPundit*;[12] the idea is that people can rely on *InstaPundit*'s assessment of other weblogs, without having to take time themselves to work through hundreds of weblogs. Within the field of library and information science, there are professional weblogs that serve this function – for example, *Library Stuff*.[13] While this strategy can work for individuals, for librarians who are assesing weblogs as part of their job it should be only a starting point. For librarians to rely totally on an outside expert to guide them through the 'blogsphere' would be like handing over the library's book purchasing or collection development policy to an outside body.

Sooner or later, both the individual web surfer and the professional librarian will have to make some decisions about weblogs. 'Yes, there's ... a lot of chaff out there, and it's the reader's responsibility to sift and choose'.[14] And it is the librarian's responsibility to make choices on behalf of others. Just as for selecting books or Internet resources, the use of stated selection criteria will help to ensure that decisions are informed and consistent. There are currently no widely accepted criteria for the evaluation of weblogs. The following are based on standard library selection criteria that have been adapted for assessing Internet resources.[15] They incorporate criteria for assessing the content of the weblog, criteria for assessing the features associated with online resources and criteria related specifically to the characteristics of weblogs. An indication is given, under each heading, of some of the questions that might be asked in order to assess the weblog.

Not all these criteria will be appropriate for every weblog. In addition, a negative answer to a question may not represent a disadvantage – for example, no one expects the website of a political party to present a balanced or unbiased view of an issue; people go to such a weblog to get the point of view of the particular political party.

Criteria for evaluating information weblogs

Criteria for assessing information content

Authority

- Who is responsible for the information content?
- What is known of their qualifications or expertise or reputation in their field?
- What organisation (if any) is behind the weblog as sponsor or publisher?
- Does the weblog provide information about the creator or sponsor (for example, through a 'Who are we?' link)?
- Is the weblog listed by reliable directories or reference sites?

Purpose

- What is the aim or purpose of the weblog? Who are the intended readers?
- Is that aim or purpose aligned to the needs of users?
- To what extent is the aim or purpose achieved through the weblog?

Scope and coverage

- Is the intended scope and coverage made clear?
- Is the scope and coverage aligned to the aim or purpose of the weblog?
- Is the scope and coverage aligned to the needs of users?
- How comprehensive is the coverage of the topic? Are there any gaps in coverage?

- How deep is the coverage of the topic? Is the coverage more deep in some areas than others?
- Are there references to other sources of information on the topic? What is the quality of those sources?

Reliability

- How accurate is the information?
- Can the information be verified through other sources?
- Does the content reflect a particular point of view? Is there any evidence of bias?
- Is the information presented in a way that inspires confidence? Are there any spelling errors or grammatical errors? What is the quality of the writing?
- Are sources of content documented and referenced?

Currency

- How often is the weblog updated?
- How comprehensive are the updates?
- Is the information current?
- Are photographs and other visual features current?

Criteria for assessing features associated with online resources

Format

- How appropriate is the format of the weblog, bearing in mind the aim or purpose and the intended audience?
- How appropriate is the format of the weblog, bearing in mind the subject?
- Is the weblog site laid out clearly? Is it well organised?

Appearance

- How attractive is the main page? What impression does it give to the reader?
- Is the appearance in alignment with the aim or purpose, the content and the intended audience?
- Is colour used appropriately for font face, links, background?
- Is the size of the font appropriate given the aim or purpose and the intended users?

Navigation

- Is the site easy to navigate?
- Are navigation features consistent throughout the site?
- How easy is it to find an item of information that should be on the site?
- Is there a site map or some indication of how the site is structured?
- Can users search the site? If so, how well does the search engine work and how easy is it to use?

Links

- Are the links relevant and appropriate given the aim or purpose and the intended users?
- Are the links working?
- Are the links the best available on the topic?
- Are the links described in an appropriate way?
- Is it easy for readers to distinguish links from the content of the weblog itself?

User needs

- Can the weblog site be used by people with vision problems? Does the site work with assistive technology such as screen readers for the blind?
- Are the needs of physically handicapped users accommodated?
- Is there any evidence of usability testing of the site?
- Is the weblog site publicly available for all users? Do parts of the site require payment? Is access to all or some of the site restricted by password?

Technical aspects

- Does the weblog site work well in any browser? Does it work well in older browsers as well as in current software?
- Does the site load quickly?
- Is the site available most of the time, or are there periods when it is down?
- Do users need to scroll through long pages?
- How well do the pages print out? If the pages are complex, is a 'print format' available?

Criteria related specifically to weblogs

Appeal as a weblog

- How appealing is the weblog in comparison with other weblogs on the topic?
- How well does the weblog use the standard features of weblog software?

Arrangement by date

- Are weblog posts dated? Is there a time signature on each post?
- Is it clear how often the weblog is updated?
- Is the update schedule appropriate to the aim or purpose and the topic?

Interactivity

- What interactive features are available on the weblog? How well do they work?
- Are the interactive features used? How many people post comments and how often?
- Are the comments relevant to the aim or purpose of the weblog, the subject coverage and the audience?
- Are the people who are commenting representative of the intended audience?
- How easy is it for readers to post comments or interact with others through the weblog?

Features

- Is an archive provided? How easy is it to find older posts or comments?
- Does the weblog use permalinks (permanent links) to identify each post?
- Are webcams or other similar features relevant and appropriate?
- Is there an RSS feed? How easy is it to find information about the feed?

In the following sections, lists are provided of selected weblogs in particular subject areas, including the social sciences, books and reading, news and current events, and technology, plus some other weblogs of interest.

Selected weblogs: the social sciences

Within the broad field of the social sciences, there are many significant weblogs, most maintained by experts in their subject field. The list below includes weblogs from education, literacy and information literacy, law, and electronic publishing, among others. Other social science fields (such as sociology, anthropology, psychology) also have well-known and respected weblogs.

EdBlogger Praxis

http://educational.blogs.com/edbloggerpraxis/

EdBlogger Praxis is devoted to the use of weblogs in education at all levels from kindergarten to postgraduate. The authors (listed on the blog) include teachers in schools, faculty members in universities and editors of professional journals and newsletters. Most are in the United States. There are links to weblogs used in university and college teacher education courses, to weblogs created as classroom activities in elementary and secondary schools, and to the personal weblogs of teachers.

Information Literacy Weblog

http://ciquest.shef.ac.uk/infolit/

Sheila Webber of Sheffield University in the United Kingdom maintains this weblog for 'sharing relevant items and information relating to information literacy worldwide' (from the masthead). It provides commentary on, and links to, articles, reports, conferences, projects and international initiatives.

Jerz's Literacy Weblog

http://jerz.setonhill.edu/weblog/index.jsp

American academic Dennis G. Jerz provides annotated links to Internet resources (articles, essays, web pages) related to writing and to literacy. 'Literacy' is interpreted broadly to include information literacy. In addition, there is some coverage of aspects of information technology that affect Internet users (for example, spam).

JURIST: The Paper Chase

http://jurist.law.pitt.edu/paperchase/

Edited by Professor Bernard Hibbitts and 'some 30 law students', this weblog comes from JURIST, the non-commercial legal information and legal education web portal at the University of Pittsburgh School of Law in the United States. The team provides daily summaries of legal news stories of general interest, with links to related online resources. The material is 'carefully selected for legal significance, quality and authoritativeness'.

Keeping Legal

http://www.keepinglegal.com/

Produced by Paul Pedley (London, England), editor of *Keeping Legal*, this weblog covers 'legal issues affecting the information profession'. Topics include copyright, digital rights management, data protection, freedom of

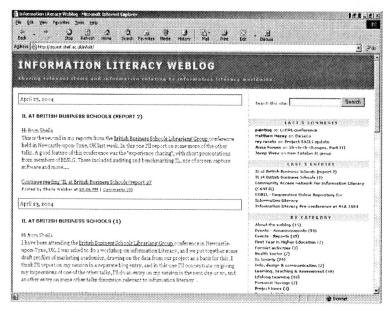

Figure 2.1 The *Information Literacy Weblog* from Sheffield University, UK

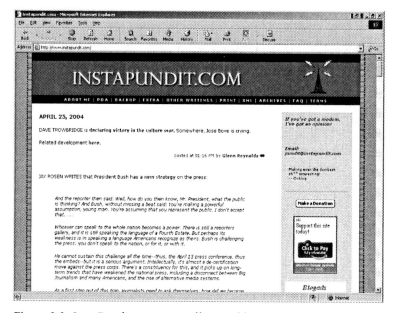

Figure 2.2 *InstaPundit*, a current affairs weblog

information, intellectual property, electronic commerce, legal deposit, privacy issues and UK politics and government.

Privacy Digest

http://PrivacyDigest.com/

From Paul Hardwick, this is 'your daily source for news that can impact people's privacy'. Coverage includes privacy and civil rights, privacy on the Internet, background credit checks, credit card privacy, electronic voting, caller ID.

Scholarly Electronic Publishing Weblog

http://info.lib.uh.edu/sepb/sepw.htm

Charles W. Bailey Jr, Assistant Dean for Digital Library Planning and Development at the University of Houston (USA), has been maintaining the Scholarly Electronic Publishing Bibliography since 1996; updates have been distributed via electronic mail and the Web. In mid-2001, the weblog was established 'to provide current information about relevant new books, journal articles, and related resources between updates of the Scholarly Electronic Publishing Bibliography'.

SiT Serious Instructional Technology

http://instructionalTechnology.editthispage.com/

With the motto 'in search of quality', this weblog covers instruction, instructional technology, instructional design and the applications of weblogs in education. All kinds of weblog-related topics come up, usually from an educational perspective – for example, RSS.

Selected weblogs: books and reading

Weblogs related to books, reading and publishing have been popular; some are the electronic equivalent of book clubs or reading circles, where an 'online community' of people discuss the books they are reading. Chapter 5 will show that a few libraries have created weblogs of this type. The weblogs listed below generally aim for a wider audience of English-speaking readers.

Arts & Letters Daily

http://www.aldaily.com/

'A service of the Chronicle of Higher Education', *Arts & Letters Daily* provides international coverage of literature, the arts and social commentary, under the headings 'Articles of Note', 'New Books' and 'Essays and Opinion'. The style of presentation is distinctive, with a well-written short summary/teaser for each item, followed by a link to the source.

BookNotes

http://booknotes.weblogs.com/

The masthead banner proclaims the coverage of this weblog as being 'books, libraries, preservation, digital convergence, music, politics', and that just about sums it up. Craig Jensen provides interesting commentary on, among other things, conferences and meetings, the future of the book and the policies of United States President George W. Bush.

Bookslut

http://www.bookslut.com/blog/

Bookslut itself is a 'monthly webzine dedicated to those who love to read'; the collaborative weblog supports and updates the webzine and provides a forum for discussion. Content includes books, authors and reviews with links to newspaper articles and other sources. Editor-in-chief is Jessa Crispin (Austin, Texas); the 'English Bookslut' is Mike Atherton, and there are other contributors (including contributors from other countries), all named on the site.

The Reading Room

http://faculty.etsu.edu/tolleyst/weblog/blogger.html

Rebecca Tolley, Librarian and Assistant Professor at East Tennessee State University, writes about what she and her readers are reading. The blog includes reviews and discussion of books and links to information about authors.

Selected weblogs: news and current events

The weblog format, which highlights the most recent posts, is particularly suitable for presenting news and information about current events. The list below includes weblogs created by traditional news organisations and weblogs created by alternative news sources. Some, like *The Billblog* and *An Unsealed Room*, are the work of individuals. Not all the bloggers are journalists.

The Billblog

http://billverity-networks.com/billslog/

Bill Thompson has been a pioneer of new media in the United Kingdom, where he established the *Guardian's* New Media Lab in the mid-1990s. He now works as a writer and journalist, specialising in new media and information technology. His weblog covers such topics as e-democracy in long and thoughtful articles with links and comments.

Cursor

http://www.cursor.org/

Cursor Inc. is an American 'tax-exempt charity that educates the public on the relationship between media and society through two free web sites', one of which is the *Cursor* weblog. It covers politics and the media, providing commentary on the 'mainstream' media and information from independent news sources. The target audience includes journalists, students, researchers and the general public.

Drudge Report

http://www.drudgereport.com/

This well-known independent news site has been credited with breaking a number of stories in the United States, including the Monica Lewinsky/Bill Clinton story. *The Drudge Report* has a style of its own, instantly recognisable despite being imitated frequently.

Guardian Unlimited: The Weblog

http://www.guardian.co.uk/weblog/

From the United Kingdom newspaper the *Guardian*, this weblog complements the print newspaper but can nevertheless be read alone for its roundup of 'best links from around the web', plus annotated links to news stories and other information on the Web. One of the things that distinguishes this weblog is the inclusion of additional information and follow-up on stories in the newspaper and on the Web. The coverage is international.

InstaPundit

http://www.instapundit.com/

This is a very active weblog, with lots of comment and discussion. It covers current events around the world, reports of censorship, Internet news and news of interest to the blogging community. It has a long list of good current events and opinion weblogs. A site search engine is provided.

Onlineblog (Guardian Online)

http://www.onlineblog.com/

Another weblog from the *Guardian* in the United Kingdom. It covers news about the Internet and technology in general, with some 'off topic' but interesting entries. There are summaries of news, links to news stories and Internet resources, and comments.

An Unsealed Room: A Window on Life in Israel

http://allisonkaplansommer.blogmosis.com/

An American Jewish woman living in Israel writes about day-to-day life (suicide bombers, television programmes, snow on the Golan Heights), Israeli politics, the media, the security fence and events back in the United States. The coverage is often unexpected. For example, we get two different views of the first woman to carry out a terrorist attack – a woman who 'always wanted to be the first woman who sacrifices herself for Allah' as against an 'adultress' who was forced by Hamas to carry out the suicide bombing as a form of punishment.

voxpolitics

http://www.voxpolitics.com/

This United Kingdom weblog is part of a 'campaign to explain how new technology changes politics'. The first phase was a web and e-mail project, sponsored by, among others, the Stationery Office, to accompany the 2001 General Election campaign. In 2002, the project entered its second phase, with the *voxpolitics* e-democracy weblog and an accompanying e-mail newsletter. Posts from early 2004 report on meetings about the political potential of weblogs and discuss the weblogs of parliamentarians and London city councillor Lynne Featherstone.

Watchblog: 2004 US Election News and Opinion

http://www.watchblog.com

Watchblog is divided into three sections: one for the Democrats; one for the Republicans; and one for all other parties and candidates. Each of the sections has its own editor, and 38 political writers contribute to the weblog. There are articles and commentary on important speeches and the primary contests, plus links to Internet sources.

Where is Raed?

http://dear_raed.blogspot.com/

This is the online journal of 'Salam Pax', the 'Baghdad logger' of the war in Iraq. The weblog entries commenced not long before the invasion of Iraq and the weblog is still being maintained. As a result of the weblog, both Salam Pax himself and his friend Raed have become Web celebrities.

Selected weblogs: technology

There are an enormous number of weblogs in the fields of science and technology, and particularly in the field of computer-related technologies. Some, like *SciTech Daily*, are broad-based services that cover developments around the world; others, such as the *Google Weblog*, are much narrower in focus.

Corante Tech News, Filtered Daily

http://www.corante.com/

'Corante is a leading news service on technology', compiled by a group of expert editors. Longer articles as well as short pieces, news and interviews deal with weblogs, weblog technology, the relationship of weblogs to the World Wide Web in general and issues associated with weblogs and blogging, plus communications, e-business and policy.

Financial Applications Security Weblog

http://radio.weblogs.com/0103213/

From Pelle Braendgaard, this weblog charts 'the latest standards, software and policies affecting the security of financial applications'. All the different components of systems are covered. There are links to the various reports, standards, articles and other documents that are discussed.

Google Weblog

http://google.blogspace.com/

A forum for postings and discussion on all things related to Google, plus news of new developments from the Google engineers. A useful way to keep up to date with changes at this important search engine.

SciTech Daily

http://www.scitechdaily.com/

SciTech Daily was established under Managing Editor Vicki Hyde as a sister site to the very successful *Arts & Letters Daily* (see above). 'The idea was to link to the most thought-provoking, well-researched online items in the world of science and technology'. Material is added most days under the headings 'Features and Background', 'Books and Media' and 'Analysis and Opinion'.

Slashdot

http://slashdot.org/

'News for nerds. Stuff that matters' is the masthead slogan of this weblog. And indeed, *Slashdot* delivers, with large numbers of posts and with sometimes hundreds of people commenting on each post. There is a book review section, to which readers can contribute their own reviews, and a section of 'quick links' to 'cool sites'.

Techdirt

http://www.techdirt.com/

Discussion of all kinds of issues related to information technology, with links and comments. Topics covered include wireless access to the Internet, spam, online films, camera phones, RSS, hacking, music downloads, Internet filtering software, computer viruses and more. *Techdirt* also provides corporate intelligence for 'enterprise blogs' on the intranets of companies or other organisations.

Technology Review: MIT's Magazine of Innovation, Daily Weblog

http://www.technologyreview.com/blog/index.asp

News summaries and comment, with links to the original stories. All types of technology are covered, from space exploration to MP3 and other aspects of the Web. The weblog has good coverage of the social impact of new technologies.

WiFi Networking News

http://wifinetnews.com/

A site for 'daily reporting on Wi-Fi and the whole IEEE 802.11 family of standards'. Coverage includes protecting WiFi networks, new WiFi products, wireless broadband and other topics in this fast-moving field. The weblog also provides an interactive 'hotspot locator'.

Other weblogs

The following weblogs form a miscellaneous group. The topics are varied and the sites serve different purposes. What they have in common is that all have been well reviewed in online or print journals. Included are some personal weblogs that are significant either because of the identity of the blogger or because of the subject coverage of the weblog.

Boing Boing

http://boingboing.net

Boing Boing is subtitled 'a directory of wonderful things'. From Cory Doctorow, it is an idiosyncratic collection of unusual stories and links, culled from around the Internet. Here you will find current events, cartoons, weird images, computer stuff and stories about music, movies, sculpture, sport and life in cyberspace.

Going Underground's Blog

http://www.london-underground.blogspot.com/

This weblog, compiled by Annie Mole, is a companion to the *Going Underground* website that provides information about travelling on the London Underground. The weblog takes the form of a London Tube diary, with stories, links and photographs. It is informative and, above all, fun.

Megnut

http://www.megnut.com/

Meg Hourihan was among the first bloggers, beginning in 1999 at a time when blogging was largely a male activity ('I am woman, hear me blog'). She co-founded the web technology group Pyra and was co-creator and director of development for Blogger, the pioneering weblog software. On *Megnut* she writes about what she is reading, life in New York City – in other words, this is a personal weblog from someone who has been involved in blogging for a long time as these things are measured.

Náttúruvaktin/NatureWise

http://www.natturuvaktin.blogspot.com/

An Icelandic weblog devoted to natural science, the conservation of resources and related political, social and economic issues. There are annotated links to Internet resources in English and other languages as well as in Icelandic. Among the issues canvassed are the building of the Karahnjukar

Dam and whaling in the North Atlantic, both important and controversial in Iceland.

The next chapter (Chapter 3) deals with tools (primarily directories and search engines) and techniques for finding weblogs, regardless of the topic. Chapter 4 covers weblogs in just one field, library and information science, giving some idea of the enormous number and range of weblogs that are available in any subject field.

References

1. Belinda Weaver, 'Weaver's Web', *InCite* Sep. 2003 (available at *http://www.alia.org.au/publishing/incite/2003/09/weaver .html* accessed 8 Oct. 2003).
2. Martin Wolk, 'Business Pros Flock to Weblogs', *MSNBC* 15 Apr. 2002 (available at *http://www.msnbc.com/news/737986 .asp?cp1=1* accessed 16 Apr. 2002).
3. Hazel D'Aguiar, 'Weblogs: The New Internet Community?', *CILIP Update* 2.1 (2003): 38–39.
4. *http://info.lib.uh.edu/sepb/sepw.htm*
5. *http://ciquest.shef.ac.uk/infolit/*
6. *http://www.guardian.co.uk/weblog/*
7. *http://jurist.law.pitt.edu/paperchase/*
8. James D. Miller, 'Blogging: An Economist's View', *TCS Tech* 12 Apr. 2002, online (available at *http://www .techcentralstation.com/1051/techwrapper.jsp?PID=1051-250&CID=1051-041002C* accessed 12 Apr. 2002).
9. *http://dear_raed.blogspot.com/*
10. See *http://www.fairvue.com/awards2004/.*
11. James D. Miller, 'Blogging: An Economist's View', *TCS Tech* 12 Apr. 2002, online (available at *http://www .techcentralstation.com/1051/techwrapper.jsp?PID=1051-250&CID=1051-041002C* accessed 12 Apr. 2002).
12. *http://www.instapundit.com/*
13. *http://www.librarystuff.net/*

14. Charles Cooper, 'When Blogging Came of Age', *CNET News.com* 21 Sep. 2001, online (available at *http://news.cnet .com/news/0-1272-210-7242676-1.html* accessed 19 Oct. 2001).

15. See, for example, 'Evaluating Information Found on the Internet' from the Sheridan Libraries at Johns Hopkins University (available at *http://www.library.jhu.edu/elp/useit/ evaluate/index.html* accessed 11 Mar. 2004); 'Library Selection Criteria for WWW Resources' from Carolyn Caywood (available at *http://www.keele.ac.uk/depts/es/ Stephen_Bostock/Internet/criteria.htm* accessed 11 Mar. 2004); 'Evaluating Internet Resources' from the University at Albany Libraries (available at *http://library.albany.edu/ internet/evaluate.html* accessed 11 Mar. 2004).

3

Finding weblogs

As Chapter 2 showed, there are weblogs that provide useful information, discussion and commentary in a wide range of subject fields. How can the potential reader locate weblogs in an area of interest? With the number of weblogs now in the millions, this is a reasonable question. However, ...

It's not easy!

Unfortunately, finding out about quality weblogs can be a matter of serendipity. There is no single print or online source of information about all weblogs. The state of the 'blogsphere' at present could be compared to the state of the World Wide Web at about the time the first web-based search engines were emerging. Some tools are available, but the coverage of even the best is far from comprehensive.

The major web-based general search engines, including Google,[1] Teoma[2] and AlltheWeb,[3] present pages from weblogs in their search results. In the listings of search results, Google sometimes identifies a page as coming from a weblog, but this cannot be relied upon in all cases. This means that a person looking for weblogs that deal with a topic usually has to inspect almost all the items in a list of search results. Although it is not a very efficient or reliable method, search results presented by the general search engines can alert a user to new weblogs. Another problem is that although Google, in particular, attempts to identify frequently updated sites (such as weblogs) for more frequent 'crawls' to update the Google indexes, it is still very unlikely that the current weblog posts will be indexed. In addition, it is possible that a post that was indexed by a search engine while it was on the main page of the weblog will have moved to the weblog's archive before the search engine's crawler visits the site again.

Rather more effective are the directories provided by the web-based search engines such as Yahoo![4] and Google that present lists of weblogs categorised in various ways. Nevertheless, these directories contain only a relatively small proportion of the total number of weblogs in existence.

This chapter will discuss some specialist tools for identifying weblogs in a subject area. These tools include directories and weblog search engines, among others. Readers should bear in mind that this is a very new field, and new finding tools and sites are emerging all the time. Some don't survive very long, others have stayed around for a while and a few are improving quite rapidly.

Directories of weblogs

In general, the directories of weblogs take one of two forms: general directories (covering weblogs in all subject areas); and subject-specific or targeted directories. The latter may cover weblogs that deal with a particular subject or topic, weblogs that come from a particular country or region or weblogs in a particular language. Some directories are evaluative, that is they claim to list only quality weblogs. Others simply present a list with no indication of how or why the list was compiled. Indeed, some are compiled automatically from the lists of recently updated blogs that are provided on weblog software sites (for example, on the Blogger[5] home page). Most of the directories also provide a search engine but the capabilities of these search engines vary a great deal. The list of 'targeted directories' below provides just a sample of what is available; it will give readers an idea of the range and variety of the directories – though most of these directories are fairly small.

General directories

Bligz

http://bligz.com/

Bligz is a weblog directory based on metadata. One of the aims of the site is 'to promote the use of metadata in the blogging community'; another is to find 'new ways to use metadata that will create useful connections between and among blogs'. Bloggers can submit their weblogs for consideration. Early in 2004, almost four thousand weblogs were listed. There is a list of 'recently added blogs'. Access is provided through an alphabetical list by weblog name, by a country listing and through a site search engine.

Blogarama

http://www.blogarama.com/

Blogarama, 'The Blog Directory', listed 8,813 weblogs in March 2004. The weblogs can be browsed by 24 subject categories (and sub-categories), or searched via a site search engine. There are lists of 'new blogs', 'most popular' blogs and 'most cool' blogs and readers can submit sites for consideration.

Blogstreet

http://www.blogstreet.com/

Blogstreet listed 144,143 weblogs and 42,183 RSS feeds as of March 2004. The search engine searches individual posts on the weblogs. The directory lists weblogs by broad topic. 'Library' is one of the topics; it produces a list of 33 weblogs in the field of library and information science, broadly speaking.

DMOZ Open Directory Project: Weblogs

http://dmoz.org/Computers/Internet/On_the_Web/Weblogs/

From the DMOZ Open Directory Project, this is a general listing of weblogs, organised alphabetically by the name of the weblog. In March 2004, 4,258 weblogs were listed with access also by subject category and by language. The DMOZ Open Directory Project provides a specialised list of library and information science weblogs (see Chapter 4) in addition to this general list.

Eatonweb Portal

http://portal.eatonweb.com/

This site, one of the first weblog directories, lists 16,788 weblogs (as of March 2004) in 87 categories such as 'Personal', 'Humour' and 'Commentary'. It also provides listings by language and by country. There is a 'Top 50' list, a list of 'recently updated' weblogs, a list of 'new additions' and a 'random weblog' button. Users can submit weblogs for consideration.

Globe of Blogs

http://www.globeofblogs.com/

In March 2004, 9,612 weblogs were registered on *Globe of Blogs*. The directories can be browsed by weblog title, by location (by continent and then by country), by the name of the blogger or by topic. For the latter, 18 broad subjects or topics are used as the base classification, including topics like 'Arts and Entertainment', 'Careers and Occupations', 'Computers and the Internet', and 'Food and Cooking'. There is a list of recent updates and a 'random weblog' button.

Guardian Unlimited: The Weblog

http://www.guardian.co.uk/weblog/

One of the weblogs of British newspaper the *Guardian* has a 'weblog guide' with annotated lists of weblogs and directories of weblogs. The lists include 'British Blogs', 'World Weblogs', 'News Weblogs', 'Tech Weblogs'.

The Page of Only Weblogs

http://www.jjg.net.portal/tpoowl.html

An idiosyncratic, eclectic list of weblogs, categorised under headings like 'faves', 'ye olde skool' and 'journal-istic'. Unfortunately, it lists fewer than 300 weblogs. It was last updated in October 2000 but it remains online because 'it has become a subject of some historical interest', according to a note on the page.

Yahoo! Directory of Weblogs

http://dir.yahoo.com/Computers_and_Internet/Internet/World_Wide_Web/Weblogs/

Weblogs are listed in catagories such as 'Art', 'Business', 'Computers and Technology' and 'Entertainment'. There is an alphabetical listing by name of weblog (with a short annotation for each weblog), plus a listing of 'most popular' weblogs.

Targeted directories

Ageless

http://jenett.org/ageless

Ageless brings together the weblogs of 'silver-haired bloggers', categorised by year and decade of birth. Information provided includes the name of the weblog, the name of the blogger and the blogger's date of birth. 'We're sending the message that the personal, creative side of the web is diverse and ageless', says the main page of the site.

Australian Weblogs

http://www.anthonyjhicks.com/aussieblogs

A directory of Australian weblogs categorised by state or territory. There is a list of 'recently updated Australian blogs', 'updates in the last six hours' (and in the last 7–12 hours, 13–24 hours and 24–48 hours) and 'recent additions'. In March 2004, 295 weblogs were being checked daily, 162 weekly and 424 monthly.

Blogs4God

http://www.blogs4god.com/

This site is both a weblog and a directory of Christian weblogs. In March 2004, 997 weblogs were listed in eight categories, including 'Church Polity', 'Journals', 'Metablogs' and 'Techblogs'.

Javablogs

http://www.javablogs.com/

A weblog that also acts as a 'community' and directory of weblogs that have information about or discussion of the Java programming language. The weblogs are listed in alphabetical order by the name of the weblog. There are also lists of 'recent blogs' and weblogs that have been updated recently. A site search engine is provided.

NYCBloggers.com

http://www.nycbloggers.com/

This site lists 3,293 weblogs (as of March 2004) according to the New York City subway station closest to where the blogger lives. The list can be browsed by location (via an interactive map of New York City), via a diagram of the subway lines or by borough. Users can submit their weblogs for consideration. The site is nicely designed and full of interesting features. Other cities including Los Angeles[6] (USA) and Montreal[7] (Canada) have similar listings.

Pepys

http://pepys.akacooties.com/

Pepys is a directory of weblogs (and some other sites) that are created in a particular format, the diary format.

The main page says the site is 'a happy little index of blogs, diaries and journals from around the world'. The arrangement is geographical – by continent and then within that by country. Readers can submit a site for consideration. In March 2004, 3,394 weblogs and diaries were listed.

Update directories

'There are sites like *Weblogs.com* and *blo.gs* as well as others that are usually notified automatically by weblog software when a new entry is posted. Because of that they are a good way of (randomly) finding new weblogs,' says Geoffrey A. Fowler.[8] They track updates to thousands of weblogs and list them with the most recently updated first. 'Every hour you're certain to find dozens of blogs you've never heard of showing up at the top.'[9] Some of these sites offer additional features, such as customised listings for those who register or lists of 'most popular weblogs' or other listings.

Blo.gs

http://www.blo.gs/

The *blo.gs* site enables users to create a listing of their favourite weblogs and to monitor updates via *blo.gs*. In March 2004 the site claimed to be 'tracking 1,460,378 blogs for 5,490 users'.

Bloglines

http://www.bloglines.com/

Bloglines (mentioned in the previous chapter) is a free web-based service that enables users to bring together the RSS feeds of their favourite weblogs and to read them from within *Bloglines*. In addition, the *Bloglines* home page provides a list of 'top blogs' (updated daily) and a list of 'new blogs' (also updated daily). These lists are based on the feeds brought together by the users of the *Bloglines* service. The total number of weblogs listed in March 2004 was 96,710.

Weblogs.com

http://www.weblogs.com/

This site lists thousands of 'recently updated weblogs' by time of day with the most recently updated first. Although the page carries an advertisement for a particular weblog software package, the weblogs listed have been created with many different kinds of software. Browsing the list can lead to some interesting discoveries, since the only thing that the weblogs on the list have in common is that they were updated 'today'.

Search engines for weblogs

Several specialist weblog search engines are now available, but none searches even the majority of weblogs (assuming that the estimates of the number of weblogs in existence, quoted in Chapter 1, are not too far wide of the mark). While two of the search engines, Technorati and Waypath, claim to be searching more than a million weblogs, they are searching the individual posts on those weblogs, not searching for a weblog that deals with a topic. Once this is understood, search strategies can be developed that will help to identify weblogs in a subject area.

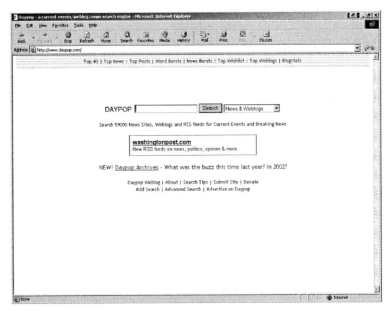

Figure 3.1 Daypop, a weblog search engine – the home page

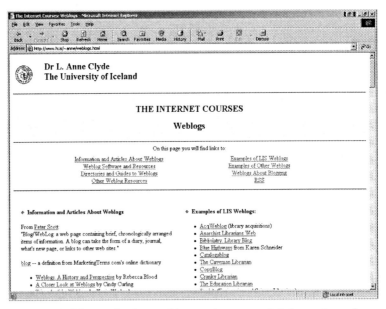

Figure 3.2 The author's teaching web page of information about weblogs (incorporating a directory of weblogs in the field of library and information science), University of Iceland

Daypop

http://www.daypop.com/

A specialist search engine that can be used to search weblogs, news sources, RSS headlines or RSS posts (or combinations of these). Simple and advanced search modes are available. The advanced search mode provides for search results to be limited by language and country. Results are returned in order of relevance. The 'Daypop Top Weblogs' is a ranked list of weblogs, the ranking based on the importance and number of weblogs that link to each weblog. Bloggers can submit their weblogs for addition to the Daypop database. In March 2004, Daypop searched 41,244 weblogs, plus other sources. Daypop also has its own *Daypop Weblog*.

Technorati

http://www.technorati.com/

Technorati was 'watching' 1,883,320 weblogs in March 2004. It bills itself as a 'conversation engine'. It finds topics that are discussed in weblog postings. It also finds weblogs that link to a particular weblog – it searches what it calls the 'cosmos' of any weblog, creating a list of other blogs that have linked to it in the previous 24 hours. In this sense, it functions rather like a citation index in the print environment, showing the 'contextual surroundings of a weblog'. Users can set up their own 'watchlist' on the system (results delivered by e-mail) or they can subscribe to an RSS feed. Both these services require a small annual fee. Users can request that their weblogs be considered for listing.

Waypath

http://www.waypath.com/

Waypath was tracking 1,604,060 weblogs as of March 2004. Searches of weblog posts can be undertaken by keyword, by name or by using a number of other fields. Waypath also has its own weblog.

Other strategies

Weblog software sites

Some of the websites maintained by the weblog software companies provide lists of the weblogs that have been created using their software. These listings may or may not be complete; some only list recently updated weblogs. Some weblog hosting companies also provide lists of the weblogs on their service. The short list below provides some examples.

Blogger

http://www.blogger.com/

Blogger has a constantly updated list of 'The 10 most recently updated blogs', a list of 'Blogs of Note' and a list of 'Fresh Blogs'.

Movable Type

http://www.movabletype.org/

The informative Movable Type home page provides a list of 'recently updated' weblogs; there are also some weblogs discussed in the text on the home page.

Tripod Blog Builder

http://blog.tripod.lycos.com/

The Tripod website provides a list of 'most recently updated' blogs and a 'Blog Directory' organised under 33 headings, from 'autos' and 'business' to 'weather' and 'women'.

Lists provided on weblogs

'Once you've found some blogs you like, following their advice is one of the best ways to find new ones.'[10] Bloggers often refer to, or list, each other. Most weblogs have a list of links to other recommended weblogs or weblogs that deal with the same topic; this is often called a 'blogroll', and using these lists to move from weblog to weblog is called 'blogrolling'. The lists also help people to explore the communities of interest that develop around a weblog. For news and current events, *InstaPundit*[11] provides a long and useful list. Many of the weblogs in the field of library and information science that are mentioned in the next chapter have substantial lists of weblogs in their field; *Library Planet*[12] and *The Shifted Librarian*[13] are good examples.

Meta sites about weblogs

Just as the Internet has been a major source of information about the Internet over the years, so weblogs and sites that focus on weblogs (meta sites) have been a major source of information about weblogs since 1999. With many new weblogs being created daily, and with the best weblogs being updated at least daily, there is ample scope for news services that keep track of new weblogs or changes to existing weblogs. There are also services that trace relationships among weblogs or track the way in which stories 'travel' through the 'blogsphere'. The following short list indicates some useful meta sites about weblogs.

Blogdex

http://blogdex.net/

Blogdex bills itself as 'the weblog diffusion index'; it tracks information 'currently spreading in the weblog community' – the stories and the weblogs on which those stories appear. Created by Cameron Marlow at the Massachusetts Institute of Technology (USA), *Blogdex* ranks the popularity of links, as well as enabling the user to follow discussions across a number of weblogs.

Le Blogeur

http://www.drmenlo.com/blogeur/

From Relton DuPiniot, this is a site that lists 'some of the greatest weblogs in the world on any given day'. He watches them ('spying on various weblogs') and monitors activity using special-purpose software.

The Blog Herald

http://www.blogherald.com/

Founded by Duncan Riley in March 2003 as a resource for bloggers, this site claims to provide 'more blog news more often'. The news and links are organised under four main headings: 'blogging news' (blogging and bloggers); 'industry news' (including the latest products); 'comment' (views and opinions on news that is affecting bloggers); and 'events' (conferences, meetings). Readers can contribute links, news and comment. The site is international in coverage. There is a site search engine.

Blogosphere.us

http://www.blogosphere.us/index.php

This site focuses on tracking trends. It collects links from weblogs around the world to show 'just what it is people everywhere are talking about'. There are lists of 'four-hour trends' (very current), 'twenty-four-hour trends' and 'top weblogs'.

Blogroots

http://www.blogroots.com/

A site that has news about, and reviews of, weblogs, plus practical advice about weblogs and blogging. This is a cooperative weblog that brings together posts from other weblogs and integrates them with posts contributed by members of the group.

Blogrunner

http://blogrunner.com/

'Track thousands of conversations', says the *Blogrunner* subtitle. This site brings together the top news stories of the day, with links to the weblogs where they are discussed. The emphasis is on news and current events, but technology stories are also tracked. The site has a search engine.

Blog Tree

http://blogtree.com/

This site invites bloggers 'to register who your inspirations were in setting up your site'. Bloggers and other users will then be able to see which sites have influenced each other – to trace relationships of influence. Users of the site can also search for existing weblogs and see the weblogs they in turn inspired. By March 2004, 11,070 authors had registered 15,324 weblogs.

Weblogs: About Weblog Technology and Usage

http://radio.weblogs.com/0105673/categories/weblog/

The coverage of this weblog is exactly as its title says – it is about weblogs, the technology behind them and how they are being used. It consists of very short entries with large numbers of links.

jill/txt

http://huminf.uib.no/~jill/

A Norwegian weblog (in English) from an academic researcher whose field is networked writing and web design. Topics covered are a mixture of the personal and the professional but include web theory, search engines, the 'politics of links' and research related to all of these.

The Weblog Review

http://www.theblogreview.com/index.php

Describing itself as 'a peer to peer review of weblogs', this site was created 'so that people can find weblogs that interest them'. Reviews are written 'by many people', and while this is a strength of the site, it limits the number of weblogs that can be listed. The most recent review is always highlighted on the home page of the site.

While there are a number of tools (including search engines and directories) that will help people to locate weblogs in their area of interest, these tools are at present imprecise and cumbersome when compared with the search engines that help us to find World Wide Web resources. This means that we are more dependent upon the work of experts or experienced bloggers who maintain directories or meta resources dealing with weblogs. This situation may well change as the weblog scene matures and more people take weblogs seriously as sources of current information.

References

1. *http://www.google.com/*
2. *http://www.teoma.com/*
3. *http://www.alltheweb.com/*
4. *http://www.yahoo.com/*
5. *http://www.blogger.com/*
6. *http://www.lablogs.com/*
7. *http://www.billegible.org/yulblog*
8. Geoffrey A. Fowler, '... Find a Blog', *The Wall Street Journal Online* 18 Nov. 2002, online (available at *http://www.waxy .org/random/html/wsj_findablog.html* accessed 15 Dec. 2002).
9. Geoffrey A. Fowler, '... Find a Blog', *The Wall Street Journal Online* 18 Nov. 2002, online (available at *http://www.waxy .org/random/html/wsj_findablog.html* accessed 15 Dec. 2002).
10. Geoffrey A. Fowler, '... Find a Blog', *The Wall Street Journal Online* 18 Nov. 2002, online (available at *http://www.waxy .org/random/html/wsj_findablog.html* accessed 15 Dec. 2002).
11. *http://www.instapundit.com/*
12. *http://www.libraryplanet.com/*
13. *http://www.theshiftedlibrarian.com/*

4

Weblogs in the field of library and information science

Chapter 2 discussed weblogs as sources of information; as such, weblogs might be expected to be important in reference work and information provision in libraries. In Chapter 5, on the other hand, library weblogs (that is, weblogs created by libraries) will be discussed. However, weblogs have also become important sources of professional information within the library and information science environment, whether the weblogs are created *by* people in the profession or *for* people in the profession (or both). Not only do they bring current trends and issues to the attention of librarians and information scientists, but they can also help practitioners to keep up to date – in other words, reading and participating in library and information science weblogs can be a professional development activity. Weblogs in the field of library and information science are the focus of this chapter, and they will be considered from a number of different perspectives, based on who created the weblog and the purpose of the weblog.

An overview

'Blogs are a natural for librarians', says Paula J. Hane;[1] certainly librarians have created a number of useful and well-regarded professional weblogs. In addition, many librarians have been quick to recognise that weblogs can be important sources of opinion, information, entertainment and relaxation as well as a tool for communication. As such, weblogs have found niches within the library and information science environment. Weblogs have been created by individual librarians, by libraries and information services, by library and information science departments in universities, and by professional and community associations.

Within the broad field of library and information science, there are weblogs that provide current information about library and information science in general or about specific aspects of library and information science; the audience is mainly library and information professionals. There are weblogs that have been created by libraries and information agencies, either for their staff or for their clients. Library schools, professional associations and companies have created weblogs for members or clients. Librarians and library and information science students have been active in creating personal weblogs, many of which deal entirely or partly with professional topics. At the reference desk, weblogs on a wide range of topics may be used as sources of current information and opinion. In addition, there are weblogs about weblogs – meta tools that help us to keep up to date with this rapidly changing field.

In this chapter, information is provided about weblogs that are created and maintained by librarians, organisations and people who are experts in their various fields. Some of these weblogs are now widely acknowledged as important sources of current information, essential reading for those who wish to keep up to date with the topic covered by the weblog. Some simply provide a useful current awareness service for their readers.

General library and information science weblogs

Under this heading is grouped a number of weblogs, most of long standing as this is understood in the weblog world, that provide informed commentary on current articles, issues and news related to the field of library and information science in general. These weblogs also provide links to the original source of the story or information and links to further discussion. Examples include the following:

librarian.net – a library weblog

http://www.librarian.net/

Jessamyn West was one of the early bloggers in the field of library and information science; one way or another, she has been 'putting the rarin' back in librarian since 1993' (as the home page says). Her weblog provides comment on currrent professional issues, discussion of articles and reports, and selected links.

Library Planet

http://www.libraryplanet.com/

Library Planet provides 'news with a library focus', with coverage of a range of issues of interest to the library and information science professions, including WiFi, RSS, metadata and portals. The weblog has a list of weblogs in the field of library and information science, an archive and a site search facility.

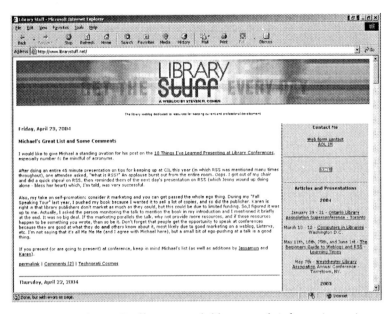

Figure 4.1 *Library Stuff*, a general library and information science weblog

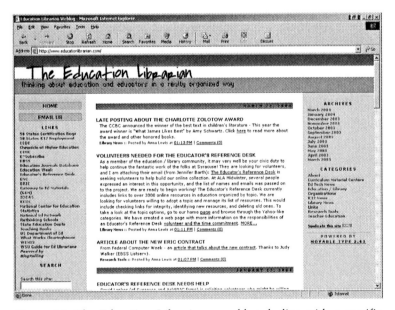

Figure 4.2 *The Education Librarian*, a weblog dealing with a specific topic in library and information science

Library Stuff

http://www.librarystuff.net/

Steven M. Cohen provides a 'library weblog dedicated to resources for keeping current and professional development'. A long list of weblogs in the field of library and information science appears on the main page.

LISNews.com (Library and Information Science News)

http://lisnews.com/

Established in November 1999, *LISNews*, a cooperative weblog, is coordinated by Blake Carver. As a team effort, it can provide more wide-ranging coverage than many of the single-person weblogs. *LISNews* has a number of special sections, including, for example, intellectual property, freedom of information, the Internet in libraries, filtering and censorship, electronic publishing and book news.

Peter Scott's Library Blog

http://blog.xrefer.com/

This weblog, from Canadian expert Peter Scott (of the University of Saskatchewan), provides good links to web-based resources, plus information about conferences and meetings, and discussion of professional issues. Peter Scott also maintains the list of 'Library Weblogs'[2] and other lists related to blogging.

Resource Shelf

http://www.resourceshelf.com/

The Resource Shelf is compiled by Gary Price to share 'resources and news for information professionals'. Daily updates provide reviews of and comment on online information resources (with links) plus comment on professional issues.

Weblogs covering specialist topics in library and information science

The specialist weblogs in the broad field of library and information science reflect the diversity and variety of the profession. There are weblogs for cataloguers, reference librarians, acquisitions librarians and library managers. There are weblogs for librarians who work in science libraries, public libraries and academic libraries. There are weblogs for librarians who are providing services via handheld computers, or who are providing services to the visually impaired, or who are testing services based on electronic books. And this just scratches the surface! Examples include the following:

The Education Librarian

http://www.educationlibrarian.com/

The focus of this weblog is 'thinking about education and educators in a really organised way'. The coverage of online and other resources in the field of education is excellent; there are links to web-based articles and reports, and reviews of books. Commercial (fee-based) online information services and databases are covered, in addition to free resources. There is an archive and links to other relevant weblogs.

EngLib (Engineering Librarians)

http://englib.info/

Catherine Lavallee-Welch, of the Laura Kersey Library of Engineering, Physical Science and Technology, University of Louisville (Kentucky), says this weblog is a way for her 'to pass along information of interest to Engineering and Science librarians'. She provides 'news about conferences, classes, professional organizations and other technological gizmos' that she finds interesting. Readers can comment on posts; there is an archive and a site search engine is also provided.

Handheld Librarian

http://www.handheldlib.blogspot.com/

This is a collaborative weblog and several of the people involved are well known in this field. The focus is, as the main page says, 'librarians sharing news, applications, and ideas of interest with others working with hand held computer technology'. Coverage includes the technology itself, new products, new projects or trials, access to online information services via handheld computers and reading electronic books via handheld computers. There are links to online resources and an archive is available.

Open Stacks

http://openstacks.lishost.com/os/

'Promoting information access and literacy for all' is the stated goal of this weblog from Greg Schwartz (Kentucky). While basically a personal diary about life in a branch library, this weblog covers issues such as censorship, computer access in libraries and collection development and weeding.

Question Authority

http://drei.syr.edu/qauthority_pub/

From the Digital Reference Education Initiative (DREI), this weblog is a place where 'various individuals in the reference community can post their thoughts on current issues in digital reference education and training' (from the main page).

SiteLines – Ideas About Web Searching

http://www.workingfaster.com/sitelines/

Created and maintained by Rita Vine (librarian, Web search trainer and lead site evaluator for the Search Portfolio Web search product), *SiteLines* has information about relevant conferences and other events, new articles and reports, search engines and materials for training Web searchers. The archive of the weblog is available for browsing and there is a site search engine.

Weblogs created by professional associations and organisations

Professional associations and other organisations have not been as active in creating weblogs as perhaps might be expected, given the involvement of individual librarians in blogging. Nor do many associations seem to have taken advantage of the features of weblogs to provide an online information update or current information service to their members. While some may be doing this on password-protected pages of their websites, their public Web pages gave no indication of this. In fact, it was surprisingly difficult to find quality weblogs that could be included in this category. Nevertheless some associations or organisations do have weblogs. Examples include the following:

Happenings

http://www.iasl-slo.org/happenings.html

Part of the International Association of School Librarianship (IASL) website *School Libraries Online, Happenings* is an online newsletter covering events around the world related to school librarianship. There is information about conferences, continuing professional development activities, new research reports, awards and prizes, and links to articles of interest (particularly in newspapers and professional journals). The use of locally written software extensions means that the format of this weblog departs from some of the 'standards' set by the specialist weblog packages. *Happenings* is edited by the IASL Webmaster, Anne Clyde.

ILA RTSF – Illinois Library Association Technology Users Group Web Logger

http://www.techusers.blogspot.com/

This weblog was established as 'a place for librarians to share the latest news, ideas on technology'. At the time of writing, there was some question about whether or not this weblog was still being maintained; the most recent post being displayed was from 2002.

MLA NewsLine

http://mla.blogspot.com/

From the Manitoba Library Association (MLA) in Canada, this weblog was designed to be an online newsletter. It seems to contain only occasional official posts from the Association. There is an archive.

While associations and organisations have not been particularly active in blogging, it says a great deal for the widespread acceptance of the weblog format (short, dated items, presented with the most recent first) that a number of professional associations have adapted this format to their website home pages as a way of drawing attention to current news and activities. For example, the Australian Library and Information Association's home page[3] incorporates a substantial section of dated announcements with links to more comprehensive information, presented with the most recent first.

Weblogs created by library and information schools

Most weblogs from library and information schools in universities have been created within specific courses and as learning experiences for the students. One of the first was the *ComLib*[4] weblog created by students in the 'Computers and Libraries' course in the Library and Information Science Department at the University of Iceland in the spring semester of 2002.[5] In the library school at San Jose State University, California, David Loertscher and Blanche Woolls were using a weblog in a course later that year. See also:

ep: the weblog

http://ep.blogspot.com/

A weblog for the course 'ep: electronic publishing' in the School of Library and Information Science at the University of Iowa in the summer of 2001. Like *ComLib*, it is no longer being maintained.

Weblogs are also being used in academic research. For example, at Griffith University's Gold Coast site in Australia, a weblog has been built primarily as a research tool for Communication and Cyber Theory; it will 'continue as a research and fact gathering blog about the phenomenon that is blogging'.[6]

Weblogs created by individual librarians

The blogging librarian is becoming a familiar character. Librarians *do* blog. Some librarians blog to share their knowledge; some blog about their professional concerns; others blog about their hobbies or their personal concerns, or about not very much at all, really. Some are serious; some are fun; some are a mixture. A number of weblogs created by individual librarians are listed above under the headings 'General library and information science weblogs' and 'Weblogs covering specialist topics in library and information science'. In addition, the following are weblogs created by librarians (or perhaps people masquerading as librarians), mostly more or less on library and information science topics (very broadly interpreted). The list is necessarily selective; there are very many more than appear here.

Barb Stripling for ALA President

http://barbstripling.net/blog/

Barb Stripling created this weblog at the end of 2003 to support her campaign to be elected President of the American Library Association (ALA). However, as Jessamyn West said on her weblog *librarian.net*[7] on 10 March 2004, 'I was sort of excited when I went to ALA and saw that ALA

Presidential candidate Barb Stripling had a blog. I was a bit less excited to see it not really go anyplace.' This is a familiar story with weblogs. It is one thing to create one; it is quite another to keep it up to date and interesting.

Confessions of a Science Librarian

http://jdupuis.blogspot.com/

John Dupuis of York University, Ontario, Canada, provides 'links and pointers to information of interest to academic science librarians' and particularly to electronic resources. He also shares his musings on a variety of library-related and other topics.

Free Range Librarian

http://frl.bluehighways.com/

'Daily meditations on librarianship' by Karen G. Schneider, the manager of *Librarians' Index to the Internet*[8] (USA). Human rights, intellectual freedom and related topics figure prominently.

Infomistress

http://www.infomistress.com/

'Tracey Friesen's site for keeping up with the info-profession' while she is 'a librarian without a library'. The coverage is wide, with some emphasis on new websites and new web-based publications. The main page has a very good list of weblogs in the field of library and information science, plus a list of blogging resources.

Lady Crumpet's Armoire

http://www.ladycrumpet.com/

This weblog is 'a digital commonplace book' of 'musings and minutiae', a twenty-first century take on the format of a couple of hundred years ago. It presents itself as 'a repository for literature, librariana, and the law. Sundries both highbrow and low' and it solicits comments from the Gentle Reader. The content is varied and includes politics, daily life at home and in the library, dealing with vendors, and the cat. The design of this weblog, with appropriate period elements, is charming.

The Laughing Librarian

http://www.laughinglibrarian.com/

Established in 1999, this weblog from Brian Smith features humour, odd stories, real-life tales ('lunacy'), news and links. There is an archive, a site search engine and a large list of weblogs (called 'groll' in this case). You can also buy the T-shirt.

Liberry Blooze

http://liberryblooze.blogspot.com/

A well-written and entertaining weblog devoted to music, CDs, DVDs, books, films, current events – and libraries. There is a long (and interesting) blogroll divided into 'librariana', 'friendlies', 'sights and sounds' and 'geekdom'.

Male Librarian Centerfold

http://www.malelibrarian.blogspot.com/

'Living better through kimchi and cataloging' says the masthead of this weblog. A librarian describes encounters with library patrons and bosses, and discusses professional issues, books and cooking.

NextGen Librarian

http://www.nextgenlibrarian.net/

In this weblog, Christine Borne (Young Adult Services Librarian at Shaker Heights, Ohio, Public Library) is 'taking librarianship to another dimension'. As she says on the main page, she provides a 'forum for library and information professionals, paraprofessionals and students in Generations X and Y to discuss the future of the profession, issues related to being a young librarian, and bring fresh perspective to all things library related'.

The Rogue Librarian

http://www.roguelibrarian.com/index.html

Carrie Bickner is the 'rogue librarian' of the title. She provides stories of life on the job, with links to a variety of resources.

Scissors and Glue

http://www.carriesullivan.net/

Scissors and glue are the 'two most frequently requested items in the library'. Carrie Sullivan writes about library users (including 'Mr Shushie', 'Obnoxious Perfume Lady' and 'Mr School of Hard Knocks') and life in general.

The Shifted Librarian

http://www.theshiftedlibrarian.com/

Jenny Levine is 'the shifted librarian'; her weblog discusses all kinds of current topics, particularly those related to information and communications technologies. She provides an archive of posts, a site search engine, a list of weblogs ('blogroll') and a mobile blogroll ('sites I read on My Treo 600').

Finding weblogs in this field

The problems associated with finding weblogs in general, as outlined in Chapter 3, are also applicable in the library and information science environment. There is no one comprehensive source of information and no one directory or search engine that will lead a reader to all relevant weblogs. To further complicate matters, the finding tools that do exist have different scope and coverage and are organised differently. However, the following, used together, will take the reader to a large number of weblogs in this field.

DMOZ Open Directory Project Library and Information Science Weblogs

http://dmoz.org/Reference/Libraries/Library_and_ Information_Science/Weblogs/

This is an alphabetical list of 392 weblogs (as of March 2004) in the field of library and information science by name of the weblogs. The single sequence includes weblogs that deal with library and information science topics, weblogs created by librarians, weblogs created by libraries, weblogs created by library school students and weblogs that deal with books. The DMOZ Open Directory Project also has a general weblog directory.[9]

Library and Information Science: Weblogs

http://www.hotels-booking-server.co.uk/travel-resources/ index.php/Reference/Libraries/Library_and_Information_ Science/Weblogs/

While it seems odd to have a directory of library and information science weblogs on a hotel booking server, this directory is nevertheless very useful. It lists weblogs in alphabetical order by title, with a screen image of each weblog's current page.

Library Weblogs (Peter Scott)

http://www.libdex.com/weblogs.html

The most comprehensive list in early 2004, this is arranged by country, and within each country, alphabetically by the name of the weblog. It includes weblogs dealing with library and information science topics, weblogs created by libraries and weblogs created by librarians, all in the one sequence.

Weblogs (Laurel A. Clyde)

http://www.hi.is/~anne/weblogs.html

This teaching web page (created for an undergraduate Internet course) provides links to information about weblogs, plus a list of weblogs in the field of library and information science, arranged alphabetically by the name of the weblog. Weblogs created by libraries are separated from the other weblogs in the field of library and information science, to suit the course aims.

As was the case with weblogs in general (see Chapter 3), one of the best ways of locating weblogs in the field of library and information science is by 'blogrolling' – following the links from one specialist library and information science weblog to another, the equivalent of following recommendations from one's peers. The *Infomistress*[10] weblog, for example, had links on the main page to around 60 library and information science weblogs at the end of 2003, while the *Open Stacks*[11] weblog had links to about the same number (but a different selection). In addition, the weblog *LIS Blogsource*,[12] 'the library weblog about library weblogs', exists primarily to draw attention to, and discuss, emerging weblogs in this field.

An important application of weblogs in the library and information science environment is the library weblog – a weblog created by a library. Library weblogs will be discussed in the next chapter, on the basis of a 2003 survey of these weblogs.

References

1. Paula J. Hane, 'Blogs Are a Natural for Librarians', *News-Link* 24 Oct. 2001, online (available at *http://www.infotoday.com/newslink/newslink0110.htm* accessed 7 Sep. 2003).
2. *http://www.libdex.com/weblogs.html*
3. *http://www.alia.org.au/*
4. *http://www.iasl-slo.org/comlib.html*
5. Laurel A. Clyde, 'Blogging Our Way Through a Course', *Personnel Training and Education* 20.1 (2003): 1–4.
6. *http://royby.com/research/weblog.php*
7. *http://www.librarian.net/*
8. *http://lii.org/*
9. *http://dmoz.org/Computers/Internet/On_the_Web/ Weblogs/*
10. *http://www.infomistress.com/*
11. *http://openstacks.lishost.com/os/*
12. *http://lisblogsource.net/*

Weblogs created by libraries: the state of the art

While weblog directories such as that of Peter Scott[1] point to a large number of useful and well-regarded weblogs that are maintained by librarians, weblogs do not seem to be so popular as an activity for libraries. Even Scott's list had more weblogs created by librarians than by libraries. An exhaustive search in October 2003 revealed only around fifty libraries with weblogs, at a time when estimates of the total number of publicly available weblogs ranged from 1.5 million to 3.4 million.[2] To provide a picture of the 'state of the art' of library weblogs (that is, weblogs created and maintained by libraries), this chapter describes a research project that looked at library weblogs as of October and into November 2003. The aims of this study were to identify the kinds of libraries that have weblogs, and to investigate the way library weblogs were being maintained, the purposes for which the library weblogs were created, the intended audience, the content of the weblogs and some indicators of commitment to the library's weblog project.[3]

Library weblogs: what the professional literature says

A review of the professional literature related to library weblogs indicates that they are generally perceived to be useful and an appropriate activity for libraries.[4] However, despite the coverage given to weblogs in mainstream newspapers and news magazines, and despite articles in the library literature that promoted the use of weblogs in libraries, Doug Goans and Teri M. Vogel found, in 2003, that few libraries actually had an official library weblog. Further, they said that most of the library weblogs they found were 'personal sites, owned by librarians whose employers do not actively promote or link to them. Some personal blogs contain links to employers, but we rarely find clear integration between a library's web presence and the blogs of its employees.'[5] This impression is supported by the author's work for a presentation on 'Weblogs in the Library and Information Science Environment' for the 'Online Information 2003' conference in London: a review of library and information science weblogs revealed more weblogs created by individual librarians than by libraries.[6]

Some writers have posited specific applications for the weblogs of libraries and information agencies. For example, Belinda Weaver suggested that a weblog could be used as a tool for communication with library users; in fact, she notes that 'It is surprising that more libraries don't use them to keep customers informed as the format is perfect for that job'.[7] She is supported by Michelle Alcock, who says 'this tool can be used to inform clients of changes, additions and news';[8] further, it can enable the library's clients to comment on the library's service. Greg Schwartz says libraries can use weblogs to provide up-to-date information on local events, to provide library news and to announce new books and other materials in the library collection. Canadian writers Geoffrey Harder and Randy Reichardt provided examples of a number of ways in which weblogs can be used by libraries to communicate with users. These include a 'parents advisory weblog' that notifies parents of additions to the children's library, a 'virtual book club or readers' advisory weblog' that provides news of books and other additions to the library collection, a 'faculty/departmental advisory weblog' in an academic library that provides news and information for instructors, and a 'services weblog' that provides information about reference services, library opening hours, and special events.[9] Some libraries have, in fact, taken up the challenge of using weblogs in this way.[10] Goans and Vogel (quoted above) have described the development of 'an official organizational blog to publicize librarywide news and events, with a hierarchy of integrated topical "sub-blogs" managed by smaller groups of librarians' for the Georgia State University Library (USA).[11] On the basis of this experience, they concluded that 'libraries and librarians need to become familiar with blogging as more of their users embrace this technology.'

Michelle Alcock suggested that weblogs could also be used to market library services.[12] Others agree with her; for example, Darlene Fichter has written an article titled 'Why and How to Use Blogs to Promote Your Library's Services'.[13] Terence K. Huwe (director of library and information resources at the Institute of Industrial Relations at the University of California, Berkeley) has described the development of a labour news weblog in his library and the use of 'blogging to market our services and make them better-known'.[14] Nevertheless, 'for much of the business community, the verdict is still out as to whether or not blogs can support marketing and financial goals. While blogging is in vogue right now, there is still some question as to its ability to build stronger brands, increase customer interaction and add to the bottom line'.[15]

Martin Roell (also quoted above) has recommended another application of weblogs – as a tool for internal communication and knowledge management within a business or organisation. In relation to knowledge management, he suggests that weblogs could be used for knowledge management within a project.[16] Darlene Fichter also believes that weblogs could be used on an intranet within an organisation such as a library as one approach to knowledge management. She says, 'Imagine teams and departments creating individual or collaborative weblogs that post sites, files, notes, and commentary. Weblogs can keep everyone in the loop and allow ideas to flow within the team and among teams'.[17] Since knowledge management applications of weblogs are generally implemented on intranets, it is not possible to study them (or even locate them) using the same techniques that are normally used to study public weblogs. However, the literature review found no reports of the successful use of weblogs in knowledge management applications in the field of library and information science.

There has, however, been some discussion of the function of a weblog as a tool for internal communication within an organisation, as recommended by Roell. For example, in an article titled 'Breaking News: Law Librarians as Newscasters',[18] Susannah Crego lists private weblogs on intranets as one tool that law librarians can use to provide information to members of a law firm. She suggests that, among other things, news feeds, streaming news reports and other RSS feeds can be provided on a private weblog, along with links to useful Internet resources and other material relevant to the interests of the law firm.

On the whole, the literature review returns an open verdict on library weblogs. Weblogs are generally perceived to be useful or potentially useful for libraries. The literature includes a few reports of 'successful' weblogs created by libraries. Nevertheless, at this stage the total literature is small and is based largely on the writings of early adopters. Few research projects have been undertaken as yet. However, given the generally positive view of the potential of weblogs in libraries, it is surprising to find that little information is available about how many libraries have created weblogs, and what the public response has been to those weblogs. The research project described in this chapter is a partial response to this need for information. Since library weblogs represent a commitment of library staff time and funds, further research is needed to answer the question of whether or not library weblogs have been worthwhile.

Investigating library weblogs

An investigation of library weblogs required that weblogs created by libraries first be identified for study. In Chapter 3 it was noted that finding out about weblogs in general can be difficult: there is no single source of information about all weblogs. Nevertheless, as Chapter 3 also showed, there are a number of search engines and directories that provide information about, and lists of, weblogs, as well as a number of other tools and strategies that can be used to locate weblogs. All were used in October 2003 to identify library weblogs but the results were disappointing. The largest specialist search engine at the time, Technorati,[19] claimed to be 'watching' 1,064,313 weblogs in October 2003. However, it failed to find any library weblogs for this project. Of the other specialist search engines, none seemed to be searching more than a small proportion of the weblogs that are estimated to be available. For example, Daypop[20] was searching '59,000 news sites, weblogs and RSS feeds', while the *Eatonweb Portal*[21] was listing '14,207 weblogs as of 10.10.03'. In addition to the national and international weblog search engines, a number of directories of weblogs were checked for library weblogs; all these directories are listed in Chapter 3. Because the specialist directories were arranged in different sequences and contained some weblogs that had not been created by libraries, all the listed weblogs were checked, those that were not created by libraries were eliminated, and the library weblogs were merged into one list of 55 weblogs. In the four weeks immediately after this work was undertaken, two more library weblogs were discovered through links on other weblogs; they were added to the list for study, making 57 in all.

The research strategy used in this project was based on the author's earlier studies of library websites.[22] The first of these studies, carried out in 1996 when library Web pages were relatively new and the professional and research literature was sparse, employed descriptive research techniques. This seemed appropriate as a way of gaining an overview of this development. Researchers looking at Web pages in other fields such as tourism and education came to similar conclusions.[23] The content analysis methodology used for the author's 1996 research has since been used as the basis for a number of other studies of Web pages; for example, Marcia J. Bates and Shaojun Lu[24] employed a similar strategy to study personal home pages, while Andrew Haines[25] used content analysis of Web pages (in addition to an e-mail survey) to investigate the personal websites of librarians. A meta-analysis carried out by Sara McMillan[26] of a number of studies that applied content analysis to the World Wide Web confirmed that content analysis was an appropriate technique for studying many different aspects of this 'dynamic environment'. Since weblogs are very much a part of the World Wide Web, and library weblogs were as new in 2003 as library home pages were in 1996, it was decided to use content analysis 'to establish a baseline describing the state of current practice'.[27]

The content analysis for this research study was based on the 57 library weblogs that were identified using the strategies described above. For each weblog, the current page was printed out in October 2003. A record was kept of the date and time of printing of each (through the date and time stamp of the printer). Some of the analyses (for example, of the countries in which the library weblogs were found) were simple counts; others were more complex. The list of weblog features was compiled by examining each printout and recording and checking each feature found. As each new printout was examined, so the list of weblog features grew. Whenever a new feature was added to the list, printouts that had already been analysed were checked again to ensure that the particular feature had not been missed previously. After all printouts had been examined, the final list of features was reviewed to make sure that the same type of feature had not been listed more than once in different ways. No attempt was made to evaluate the various features of the weblogs or to evaluate the weblogs themselves. There were two main reasons for this. First, at the end of 2003 there were no generally accepted criteria for the evaluation of weblogs or their features. Secondly, as was pointed out above, so little is known at present about library weblogs that it seemed useful to find out what was actually happening, regardless of quality issues.

Despite efforts to ensure that the study was international, library weblogs were found in only three countries: the United States, Canada and the United Kingdom, with by far the largest number (48 or 84.2 per cent) being in the

Table 5.1 Library weblogs by country

Country	Number (%)	
United States of America	48	(84.2%)
Canada	6	(10.5%)
United Kingdom	3	(5.3%)
Total	57	(100%)

United States (see Table 5.1). Given the popularity of blogging in countries like Australia, New Zealand, France and Iceland,[28] it is surprising that more countries are not represented in the list. However, checks of local search engines and professional websites in these and other countries failed to find any evidence of library blogs. This does not necessarily mean there are no library weblogs in other countries; rather that any library weblogs that may exist are inaccessible through search engines and directories.

In the United States, one public library system had three weblogs and another had two, while one university library had two weblogs. Thus the number of United States libraries with weblogs was 44. In Canada, three of the weblogs had been created by three different libraries at the University of Saskatchewan. Overall, then, the number of institutions represented by the 57 weblogs is 51.

What kinds of libraries are creating weblogs?

The largest group of weblogs (25 or 43.9 per cent) comprised those maintained by public libraries or public library systems (see Table 5.2). They were followed very closely by the group of weblogs in university or college libraries (23 or 40.3 per cent). Special libraries or research libraries

Table 5.2 Library weblogs by type of library

Type of library	Number (%)	
Public library/public library system	25	(43.9%)
Academic library (university or college)	23	(40.3%)
Special/research library	5	(8.7%)
Multi-type library network	2	(3.5%)
National library	1	(1.7%)
School board library	1	(1.7%)
Total	57	(100%)

accounted for a little less than one tenth (5 or 8.7 per cent) of the weblogs. No school library weblog was found, though there were indications that one school library in the United States had had a weblog in the past. School libraries do appear as one of the types of libraries in the Suburban Library System in Illinois (USA), along with academic libraries, public libaries and special libraries; one weblog of the Suburban Library System, *The Wide Window*,[29] provides information specifically for school and youth services librarians. However, no weblog was found for users of school libraries, though it is possible that such weblogs may exist on school intranets (where they would be inaccessible to the researcher).

Purposes for which libraries are creating weblogs

Half of the library weblogs (29 or 50.9 per cent) had some kind of statement of aims or purposes for the weblog and/or something about the intended audience. Sometimes this was just a few words; sometimes a formal statement or short paragraph. Table 5.3 presents a summary of the aims or

Table 5.3 Stated aims or purposes of library weblogs (n = 29)

Aim or purpose	Number
Provide news or information for users	20
Provide links to recommended Internet resources	9
Book reviews, information about new books	5
Provide entertainment or amusement for users	2
Provide news or information for librarians	2
Book discussions	1
Provide news or information for trustees	1
Provide research tips	1
Communication among librarians (in a library system)	1

purposes. The most common aim (in keeping with the findings of the literature review) was to provide news and information for library users: for example, the *Science News* weblog of Georgia State University 'delivers library news and information of interest to the science faculty and students at GSU',[30] while the Institute for Astronomy Library (IFA, Hawaii) weblog provides 'updates and information for IFA personnel'.[31] Another common aim was to provide users with links to recommended Internet resources: for example, the *Whittaker Live!* weblog of the Whittaker Library at the Royal Scottish Academy of Music and Drama 'provides links to useful performing arts resources on the web from the RSAMD'.[32] A number of the weblogs had more than one aim: for example, 'The St Joseph County Public Library Web Blogs will keep our patrons informed and amused with information about upcoming releases in the worlds of publishing and entertainment'[33] or 'News, links and book reviews from the Kennebunk Free Library'.[34] No library weblog was found that reflected Martin Roell's[35] recommended application of weblogs – as a tool for internal communication and knowledge management – though one, established for communication among librarians in a library system, might be seen to represent a beginning in this area.

Content of library weblogs

The contents and features of the 57 library weblogs are summarised in Table 5.4. To a certain extent the content reflects the aims and purposes of the weblogs. With a large

Table 5.4 Selected content features of library weblogs*

Content feature	Number (%)	
Name of the weblog	56	(98.2%)
Name of the library	55	(96.5%)
Date and time of posting of items	54	(94.7%)
Short articles or news items	41	(71.9%)
Links to sources of articles or news items	41	(71.9%)
Information about Internet resources	36	(63.2%)
Archives for the weblog	36	(63.2%)
Link to the home page of the library	30	(52.6%)
Statement of aims or purpose for the weblog	29	(50.9%)
RSS feed	27	(47.4%)
Information about functions/activities in the library	25	(43.9%)
Information about new books/resources in the library	20	(35.1%)
Address of the library	17	(29.8%)
Search engine for the weblog	14	(24.6%)
News from the library (e.g. about new staff)	14	(24.6%)
Link to the library catalogue	13	(22.8%)
Link to the home page of the institution of which the library is part	13	(22.8%)
Links to other weblogs	10	(17.5%)
Book reviews	10	(17.5%)
Local community news	9	(15.8%)
Library hours	7	(12.3%)
'Ask a reference question?'	7	(12.3%)
Subscribe to an e-mail newsletter from the library	6	(10.5%)
Online suggestion box	3	(5.3%)
Link to library user's own borrower account	3	(5.3%)
Link to online book club	2	(3.5%)
Disclaimer	2	(3.5%)
Link to the library's 'online community'	1	(1.7%)
Register to be notified of new content on the weblog	1	(1.7%)

* Note that this is simply a list of features that emerged from the content analysis. It should not be interpreted as a 'list of desirable features', nor should it be construed as a set of rubrics for weblog evaluation.

number of weblogs specifically aiming to provide news and updates for library users, it is not surprising to see that 41 weblogs (71.9 per cent) provided short articles and news items, with links to the original source where appropriate. Links to recommended Internet resources were provided on 36 (63.2 per cent) of the library weblogs – again not surprising, considering that providing 'links to recommended Internet resources' was the second most common aim or purpose for library weblogs. Some 25 library weblogs (43.9 per cent) provided information about functions, activities and events in the library (story time, Internet courses, author visits and so on), while 20 (35.1 per cent) provided information about new books in the library collection and/or new DVDs or access to new databases. A quarter of the weblogs (14 or 24.6 per cent) provided news about the library, for example information about new facilities or new staff members. More than three weblogs in five (36 or 63.2 per cent) had browsable archives and 14 of the weblogs (24.6 per cent) had their own search engine to assist users.

The only surprise in Table 5.4 is what it reveals as missing from the library weblogs. If we assume that one of the aims of providing a library weblog (whether that aim is articulated or not) would be to promote the library, its resources and services, then one would expect that the library (and its parent organisation) would be clearly identified and information would be provided about the library's services (or there would be links to this kind of information). Only half the weblogs (30 or 52.6 per cent) had a link back to the library's website or home page. While always necessary, such a link becomes especially important when a weblog is housed on a remote weblog hosting service such as Blogger's Blog*Spot, rather than on the library's own web server. Only 17 of the weblogs (29.8 per cent) had the street or mail address of the library. Only 13

(22.8 per cent) linked to the library catalogue; only seven (12.3 per cent) had information about the library's opening hours or links to other library services.

Providing interactive facilities designed to encourage user involvement is a strategy that is widely believed to be a way of increasing the visits (particularly return visits) to a weblog. Just over a quarter (16 or 28.1 per cent) of the 57 weblogs provided interactive facilities (see Table 5.5). At the simplest level, weblogs had a 'comment' facility that enabled users to post responses to items posted by the library staff. On only three of the eleven weblogs that provided this facility was there any evidence that users were indeed posting comments. Six of the library weblogs took interactivity a little further: a discussion forum was available. On just a few, users were able to initiate new topics or discussion threads. Since the discussion areas were usually password protected, it was impossible to get any idea of the level of user participation in discussions. An application of the discussion facility on one of the weblogs was for interaction among the staff of libraries in a library network: the messaging facility on CIIRCLS,[36] the weblog for 'communicating inside the Indian River County Library System' in Florida. However, the majority of the library weblogs (33 or 57.9 per cent) had obviously been established as a one-way medium of communication between library staff and library users or other readers of the weblog.

Table 5.5 Interactive features on library weblogs

Weblogs with interactive facilities	Number (%)	
Yes	16	(28.1%)
No	33	(57.9%)
Unclear/unknown	8	(14.0%)
Total	57	(100%)

How libraries are creating and maintaining their weblogs

Table 5.6 shows the software used to develop and maintain the library weblogs. More than 40 per cent were using Blogger,[37] and most of those were using the free version; in fact, only one seemed to be using the commercial (paid) Blogger Pro version. The next most popular weblog development software was Movable Type[38] (10 weblogs or 17.5 per cent). The only other software with more than one user was Radio UserLand[39] (5 or 8.7 per cent). Some of the weblogs for which software information was not available were almost certainly created and maintained with a system developed in-house. No libraries seemed to be using moblogging technology to maintain their weblogs, at least not on a regular basis.

Table 5.6 Library weblogs by weblog software used

Weblogs software	Number (%)	
Blogger	25	(43.9%)
Movable Type	10	(17.5%)
Radio UserLand	5	(8.7%)
Iblog	1	(1.7%)
Weblogger	1	(1.7%)
Blog-City (Blue Dragon)	1	(1.7%)
Moveable Manila: Blue	1	(1.7%)
Information not available	13	(22.8%)
Total	57 (100%)	

Some examples of library weblogs

Some examples will serve to illustrate the variety of aims, purposes, audiences, content and features of library weblogs. The Redwood City Public Library in California is using a weblog to provide information for library staff.[40] *The Wide Window* professional weblog from SLS has already been mentioned; another weblog from SLS has professional information for the librarians in all the libraries of the system – topics covered include the USA PATRIOT Act and its implications, information about conferences and conference reports, updates on legislation related to libraries and information services, and new professional books and other resources.[41] However, despite these examples of information provision for library staff in a library system, it seems that most of the other libraries that have public weblogs (for example, the National Library of Scotland[42]) are using them primarily to provide information for library users. That information might include information about Internet search engines, links to important or useful new websites, lists of new books in the library collection, or information about activities such as story times or Internet courses or author visits. Some, such as Gateshead Public Library in the United Kingdom, are also providing information about community events and issues.[43] One of the most unusual library weblogs was *Library Construction News* from the Urbana Free Library[44] in the United States; this was also designed to provide information for library users and potential users, but information related to a specific project. It provided updates on progress on a new library building, with photographs and information about access for the handicapped, changes to parking facilities (and information about public transport so library users could avoid parking problems), among other things. Something rather different is the colourful *Blogger Book Club* weblog from Roselle Public Library (USA), which provides a secure forum for 'book discussions for 4th through 6th grade patrons', with book reviews, information about authors and a page for parents.[45]

Evaluation of the library weblogs

Weblogs are generally considered to be a current information medium. The very format of weblogs highlights this current news function – the first view the user has is of the most recent posting. Most weblog development software automatically adds the date and time to each post, sometimes down to the second and sometimes even with an indication of the time zone. Some weblog sites, such as Blogger, provide a window on weblogs that have been updated within the last few minutes or even the last few seconds. Weblog search engines often use recent posts as a way of tracking and indexing weblogs – Technorati, mentioned above, is a case in point. Given this focus on recency, the frequency of updating of a library weblog can be seen as an indicator of the library's understanding of the medium and its commitment to the weblog. To get an indication of the time since the most recent update for each weblog, the date and time of the most recent posting was compared to the date and time stamp on the printout of the weblog's current page. The results are shown in Table 5.7. Only one in five of the library weblogs had been updated within the previous 24 hours. A little over half (31 or 54.4 per cent) had been updated within the previous week, but even this is pushing the envelope in weblog terms. It would be difficult, if not impossible, for example, to maintain any level of user comment or discussion on a weblog that was not updated daily. A quarter of the library weblogs (14 or 24.6 per cent) had not been updated for more than a month.

A little less than half the weblogs (27 or 47.4 per cent) provided an RSS feed. Increasingly, weblogs that provide an information service are being developed with RSS capabilities, just as news-oriented websites are, because an RSS feed is a way of bringing new readers to the site and

Table 5.7 Updating of library weblogs

Time from last update	Number (%)	
Within the day	11	(19.3%)
Within the last two days	7	(12.3%)
Within the last three days	4	(7.0%)
Within the last week	9	(15.8%)
Within the last two weeks	8	(14.0%)
Within the last month	2	(3.5%)
Within the last three months	6	(10.5%)
Within the last six months	4	(7.0%)
Within the last year	1	(1.7%)
Within the last two years	3	(5.3%)
Time of last posting not available	2	(3.5%)
Total	57	(100%)

ensuring coverage for the weblog in the directory and search sites. Apart from the benefit to the provider of the weblog (in terms of greater exposure), RSS makes possible the delivery of timely information to the computer desktops of users without the users having to take any step other than installing and configuring a news aggregator or reader. Provision of an RSS feed is generally considered to be an indicator of intent to provide a serious service via a weblog and of commitment to the weblog.

The great majority of the library weblogs in the study were in the United States. Most had been created by public or academic libraries. In general, the library weblogs were based on free or cheap and relatively unsophisticated weblog tools or services. Most had been created to provide news and information for library users and/or to provide links to recommended Internet resources, and some did this well. Nevertheless, it was disturbing that a large number of weblogs failed even to provide a link to the website or home page of their library, much less the library catalogue or reference services provided by the library. Most library

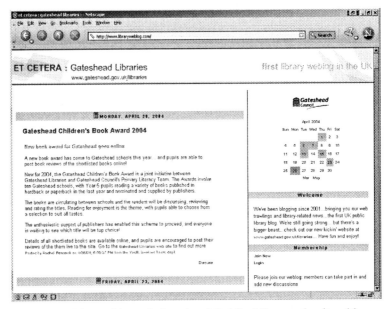

Figure 5.1 The weblog of Gateshead Public Library, the first library weblog in the UK

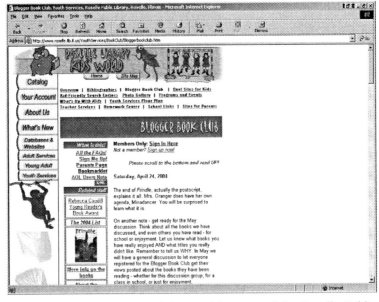

Figure 5.2 *Blogger Book Club*, a weblog created by Roselle Public Library, Illinois, USA

weblogs were designed for one-way communication between library staff and users, but a quarter provided interactive features. The level of usage of the latter was at best unclear but seems to be very low. Most libraries were not updating their weblogs daily, giving users little reason to make frequent visits to the site. Some weblogs were updated on a very irregular basis and at the time of the study some had not been updated for many months. There is no point in having a weblog that is not kept up to date. This is a medium whose strength lies in its ability to draw attention to current information. Without an RSS feed (and fewer than half the weblogs had one), any weblog is at a disadvantage unless it already has a tight-knit user community (who all know about it) and no aspirations to expand that community.

The literature review for this research project pointed to a number of writers, including Belinda Weaver[46] and Michelle Alcock,[47] who believe in the potential of weblogs for promoting libraries and their services and for communication with users. Why, then, do so few libraries seem to have established weblogs? It cannot be the cost of the software: most of the library weblogs in the study were based on free or cheap services, and a few demonstrated that these services can indeed be used to develop attractive weblogs. It cannot be the level of skills required: while creating a weblog is not as simple as the Blogger[48] home page claims ('push-button publishing for the people'), nevertheless many more librarians seem to have created professional and personal weblogs than have libraries. It could be that Weaver and Alcock are wrong, though if they are, then no articles have appeared that would show this. On the other hand, it could be that there are institutional barriers to the establishment of library weblogs, perhaps stemming from a distrust of informal sources of information.

For those libraries that have weblogs, how many have been evaluated to measure the extent to which they are meeting user needs? The literature is no help in answering this question. The general lack of user comments on those library weblogs that provided a facility for commenting suggests that users are not particularly involved with their library weblogs. Do users *want* to comment or discuss? We really don't know, but the results of this research study suggest that it is at least open to question. Or is it that the potential users don't know that the library weblog exists? Or that the users don't know *how* to comment? It is hard to tell from the evidence available.

What do users want in a library weblog? We really don't know. Is it perhaps the case that there is not yet a critical mass of library users who know enough about weblogs to understand the potential? If so, it is possible that as users become more familiar with weblogs and their applications, usage of library weblogs will increase and users may be more willing to take part in online discussions or use other interactive features of weblogs.

References

1. *http://www.libdex.com/weblogs.html*
2. Phil Wolff, 'The Blogcount Estimate: 2.4 to 2.9 Million Blogs', *Blogcount* [weblog] 23 Jun. 2003, online (available at *http://dijest.com/bc/* accessed 8 Sep. 2003). Robyn Greenspan, 'Blogging by the Numbers', *Cyber-Atlas* 23 Jun. 2003, online (available at *http://cyberatlas.internet.com/big_picture/ applications/article/0,1323,1301_2238831,00.html* accessed 11 Oct. 2003).
3. A formal report of this research will appear in 2004 as: Laurel A. Clyde, 'Library Weblogs', *Library Management* (in publication as this book was being written).

4. Blake Carver, 'Is It Time to Get Blogging?', *Library Journal* 15 Jan. 2003, online (available at *http://www.libraryjournal .com/index.asp?layout=article&articleid=CA266428& publication=libraryjournal* accessed 4 Feb. 2004).

5. Doug Goans and Teri M. Vogel, 'Building a Home for Library News With a Blog', *Computers in Libraries* 23.10 (2003): 20–26.

6. Laurel A. Clyde, 'Weblogs in the Library and Information Science Environment', *Online Information 2003 Proceedings, 2–4 December 2003, London, UK*, eds Catherine Graham, Jonathan Lewis and Alison Yates (Oxford: Learned Information, 2003) 101–106.

7. Belinda Weaver, 'Weaver's Web', *InCite* Sep. 2003, online (available at *http://www.alia.org.au/publishing/incite/2003/ 09/weaver.html* accessed 8 Oct. 2003).

8. Michelle Alcock, 'Blogs – What Are They and How Do We Use Them?', *Quill* 103.8 (2003): online (available at *http:// www.alia.org.au/members-only/groups/quill/issues/2003.8/ blogs.html* accessed 8 Oct. 2003).

9. Geoffrey Harder and Randy Reichardt, 'Throw Another Blog on the Wire: Libraries and the Blogging Phenomenon', *Feliciter* 2 (2003): 85–88.

10. Greg Schwartz, 'Blogs for Libraries', *Web Junction* 3 Aug. 2003, online (available at *http://www.webjunction.org/do/ DisplayContent?id=1432* accessed 8 Sep. 2003).

11. Doug Goans and Teri M. Vogel, 'Building a Home for Library News With a Blog', *Computers in Libraries* 23.10 (2003): 20–26.

12. Michelle Alcock, 'Blogs – What Are They And How Do We Use Them?', *Quill* 103.8 (2003): online (available at *http:// www.alia.org.au/members-only/groups/quill/issues/2003.8/ blogs.html* accessed 8 Oct. 2003).

13. Darlene Fichter, 'Why and How to Use Blogs to Promote Your Library's Services', *Marketing Library Services* 17.6 (2003), online (available at *http://www.infotoday.com/mls/nov03/ fichter.shtml* accessed 4 Feb. 2004).

14. Terence K. Huwe, 'Born to Blog', *Computers in Libraries* 23.10 (2003): 44–45.

15. Alf Nucifora, 'Blogs: The Next Frontier of Biz Communication', *Bizjournals* 17 Nov. 2003, online (available at *http:// www.bizjournals.com/extraedge/consultants/shoestring_ marketing/2003/11/17/column194.html* accessed 20 Jan. 2004).

16. Martin Roell, 'Weblogs Can Improve Business?', *Newsfox.com* 26 May 2003.

17. Darlene Fichter, 'Blogging Your Life Away', *Online* May 2001.

18. Susannah Grego, 'Breaking News: Law Librarians as Newscasters', *Law.com* 4 Sep. 2001, online (available at *http://www.law.com/* accessed 16 Mar. 2002).

19. *http://www.technorati.com/cosmos/search.html*

20. *http://www.daypop.com/*

21. *http://portal.eatonweb.com/*

22. Laurel A. Clyde, 'The Library as Information Provider: The Home Page', *The Electronic Library* 14.6 (1996): 549–558. Laurel A. Clyde, 'The School Library WebSite: On the Information Highway or Stalled in the Carpark?', *Unleash the Power: Knowledge, Technology, Diversity: Papers Presented at the Third International Forum on Research in School Librarianship, Birmingham, Alabama, USA, November 10–14, 1999*, eds Lynne Lighthall and Eleanor Howe (Seattle, WA: International Association of School Librarianship, 1999): 227–237.

23. See, for example, V. Cano and R. Prentice, 'WWW Home Pages for the Tourism Industry: The Scottish Experience', *ASLIB Proceedings* 50.3 (1998): 61–68. T. Gray, J. Romano and J. Clark, 'What's on the Menu? School Web Sites in the United States, 1998', online (available at *http://www .teacherzone.com/specialreports/onmenu/index.htm* no longer available).

24. Marcia J. Bates and Shaojun Lu, 'An Exploratory Profile of Personal Home Pages: Content, Design, Metaphors', *Online and CDROM Review* 21.6 (1997): 331–340.

25. Andrew Haines, 'Librarians' Personal Web Pages: An Analysis', *College and Research Libraries* 60. 6 (1999): 543–550.

26. Sara McMillan, 'The Microscope and the Moving Target: The Challenge of Applying Content Analysis to the World Wide

Web', *Journalism and Mass Communication Quarterly* 77.1 (2000): 80–89.

27. T. Gray, J. Romano and J. Clark, 'What's on the Menu? School Web Sites in the United States, 1998', online (available at *http://www.teacherzone.com/specialreports/onmenu/index.htm* no longer available).

28. See, for example, Robyn Greenspan, 'Blogging by Numbers', *CyberAtlas* 23 Jun. 2003, online (available at *http://cyberatlas.internet.com/big_picture/applications/article/0,1323,1301_2238831,00.html* accessed 11 Oct. 2003).

29. *http://www.sls.lib.il.us/consulting/news/thewidewindow/*

30. *http://www.library.gsu.edu/news/index.asp?typeID=56*

31. *http://ifalibrary.blogspot.com/*

32. *http://rsamd.weblogger.com/*

33. *http://homepage.mac.com/nrdtsjcpl/B1732759005/*

34. *http://kennebunklibrary.blogspot.com/*

35. Martin Roell, 'Weblogs Can Improve Business?', *Newsfox .com* 26 May 2003.

36. *http://sebastianlibrary.com/ciircls/*

37. *http://www.blogger.com/*

38. *http://www.movabletype.org/*

39. *http://radio.userland.com/*

40. *http://www.rcpl.info/services/liblog.html*

41. *http://www.sls.lib.il.us/*

42. *http://www.nls.uk/news/*

43. *http://www.libraryweblog.com/*

44. *http://urbanafreelibrary.org/bldgblog.html*

45. *http://www.roselle.lib.il.us/YouthServices/BookClub/Bloggerbookclub.htm*

46. Belinda Weaver, 'Weaver's Web', *InCite* Sep. 2003, online (available at *http://www.alia.org.au/publishing/incite/2003/09/weaver.html* accessed 8 Oct. 2003).

47. Michelle Alcock, 'Blogs – What Are They and How Do We Use Them?', *Quill* 103.8 (2003): online (available at *http://www.alia.org.au/members-only/groups/quill/issues/2003.8/blogs.html* accessed 8 Oct. 2003).

48. *http://www.blogger.com/*

6

Creating a weblog:
the options

Chapter 5 provided an overview of the 'state of the art' of library weblogs as of the last quarter of 2003. It demonstrated that, despite the potential advantages of weblogs as presented in the professional literature, relatively few libraries had created weblogs. For those libraries where the creation of a weblog is being considered, this chapter provides basic information about weblog software, weblog hosting and special features of weblogs. Chapter 7 provides information about the ongoing maintenance and management of a library weblog.

An overview of the options

There are two main (and interdependent) requirements in weblog development and maintenance: the software or system used to create the weblog and to update it; and the server (the 'host') on which the weblog is made available on the Internet. Some weblog creation services also provide weblog hosting services – for example, the popular Blogger weblog creation software also provides the Blog*Spot hosting service for people who use Blogger. Nevertheless, people using Blogger to create a weblog can choose to have their weblog 'hosted' elsewhere, including on their own web server or on the web server of their ISP (Internet service provider).

There are essentially four different blogging paths available to individuals and to organisations like libraries:

- *Path 1* – using external, web-based weblog development software and an external weblog hosting service (bearing in mind that some of the web-based weblog development services also provide weblog hosting services).

- *Path 2* – using external, web-based weblog development software but hosting the weblog on a local server.

- *Path 3* – downloading weblog development software to a local machine, creating and updating the weblog on the local machine and hosting the weblog on a local server.

- *Path 4* – using a locally developed weblog system ('roll your own') and hosting the weblog locally.

Some of the advantages and disadvantages of each path are listed in Table 6.1.

Within each of the four, some options are free and some are paid (or commercial) services. It is also possible to combine free and fee-based options – for example, to download free weblog development software, create and update the weblog on a local machine but host the weblog on the web server of a local commercial ISP.

Using an external, web-based weblog development service (whether free or commercial), downloading specialist weblog development software (whether free or commercial) or developing a weblog system on site (within the organisation) are the basic weblog creation options. All have their advantages and limitations. Different people and organisations will make different decisions, depending on their budget, the level of technical skills available and the aims and purposes of the weblog, among other factors.

Using an external weblog hosting service (whether free or commercial), hosting the weblog on the web server of a local ISP or hosting the weblog on a web server on site (within the organisation) are the basic weblog hosting options. As was the case with the weblog development options, all have their advantages and limitations. Again, different people and different organisations will make different decisions, depending on local factors.

The answer to the question, 'Which weblog path is best?' is 'It depends ...' For a library, the following are among the questions that might be asked in the decision-making process:

- Are we willing to depend on another organisation for our weblog software and weblog hosting?

- Do we want to install blogging software locally on a desktop computer?

- Will our existing web server or ISP support a weblog? If so, what are the system requirements?

- What features do we want in our weblog software or system?

- How much control do we want over the appearance of the weblog?

- How much money are we prepared to spend on our weblog(s)?

- Do we want to be able to update the weblog from computers outside the organisation?

- Do we need to have weblog usage statistics, for example a record of how many people visit the weblog and how many of those visits are return visits?

Table 6.1 Blogging paths: advantages and disadvantages of each

Blogging path	Advantages	Disadvantages
Path 1 – using a web-based weblog development service and an external weblog hosting service (bearing in mind that some of the web-based weblog development services also provide weblog hosting services).	Registering on the service and setting up a weblog takes a short period of time. When free weblog and hosting services are used, this can be a very cheap way to begin. Even the paid options are relatively inexpensive. The weblog can be created and updated from any computer that is linked to the Internet. It is not necessary to purchase any special software or equipment. There is no need for the blogger to learn about maintaining a server. It is not necessary for the blogger to have a high level of technical skills. Support is usually available from the service and/or from a user group.	The weblog owner is dependent upon both a remote weblog service and a remote hosting service; if either goes down, then there is nothing the blogger can do except wait. While most weblog development services provide a degree of flexibility, the blogger will not have complete control over the appearance of the weblog; further, the greater the weblog owner's deviation from the service's standard templates, the greater the level of technical skill needed. The service may not support some of the features the blogger would like to have. It is difficult to create a near-seamless interface between the weblog and a library website. The weblog will have a different base URL from the library website.

	Many of the weblog development services provide support for the creation of RSS feeds, making this relatively easy.	If the hosting company goes out of business, then the content of weblogs hosted on the system may be in jeopardy (unless there is a local backup).
Path 2 – using a web-based weblog development service but hosting the weblog on a local server.	Registering on the service and setting up a weblog takes a short period of time. Even the paid options for weblog development are relatively inexpensive. The weblog can be created and updated from any computer that is linked to the Internet. There is no dependence upon a remote hosting service over which the weblog owner may have no control (if a remote host goes down, the blogger has no option but to wait until the problem is solved). The weblog and the library website will have the same base URL. Many of the weblog development services provide support for the creation of RSS feeds, making this relatively easy.	A higher level of technical skills is required than for Path 1 (to set up the local server, unless the weblog is hosted on an existing website). If the weblog is hosted locally and the local server goes down, then the problem has to be solved locally, so technical support may be needed. The weblog owner will be responsible for backup of the weblog, which takes time and planning. It is difficult to create a near-seamless interface between the weblog and a library website.
Path 3 – downloading weblog development software to a local	If the software is chosen well, then it should support all or most of the	A higher level of technical knowledge is required than for Path 1 or Path 2.

Table 6.1 (cont'd)

Blogging path	Advantages	Disadvantages
machine, creating and updating the weblog on the local machine and hosting the weblog on a local server.	weblog features that the weblog owner would like to have. There will be more possibilities to customise the appearance of the weblog. With content on the local server, the weblog owner has control over the archives. It is easier to create a seamless interface between the weblog and a library website. The weblog and the library website will have the same base URL.	If the local server goes down, then the problem has to be solved locally, so technical support will be needed. The weblog owner will be responsible for backup of the weblog, which takes time and planning. The selected software must run on the in-house equipment (whether Windows, Macintosh, Linux/UNIX) which may limit choice.
Path 4 – using a locally developed weblog system ('roll your own') and hosting the weblog locally.	This path gives the organisation complete control over the software, the features of the weblog and the machine on which the weblog is hosted.	This path requires the highest level of technical knowledge and skills. Technical personnel will need to have knowledge of databases, XML and

The organisation may be able to create a weblog using software that is already available within the organisation (such as database software). The advantage of this is that no one has to learn to use a new system.

The weblog can be developed to meet specific local needs, with the highest lelvel of customisation.

Weblog features can be developed as needed.

The integration of the weblog into the website of the library can be seamless.

The weblog will have the same base URL as the library website.

scripting languages like .asp or PHP, among other things.

If the weblog owner does not have those skills, then he or she will be dependent on technical staff at every step of the process.

Ongoing maintenance costs increase with the complexity of the weblog that is built.

The costs in technical staff time will be higher than for the other paths.

No free support will be available from outside the organisation.

- What relevant expertise do we have within the organisation?

- To what kind of technical support or expertise does the organisation have access?

Another factor that should be taken into account in the decision-making process is the type of weblog that the library would like to have. Specifically, what features are important? The question then becomes: 'What weblog software or system will allow us to implement the kind of weblog we want?' The following are among the questions that might be asked:

- Do we want to have audiovisual content in addition to text? What kind of audiovisual content (images, sound, a feed from a webcam)?

- Do we want to provide the facility for users to post comments to the weblog? If yes, will comments be monitored and approved before being published on the weblog?

- Do we need a way of blocking nuisance comments (for example, use of IP address blocking to ban sources of persistent off-topic comment or to ban known spammers)?

- Will users be able to initiate discussion? Will people other than the weblog owner have posting privileges?

- Will the weblog be a collaborative effort? If so, how many people (in addition to the weblog owner) will have posting privileges?

- Do we want to provide for other forms of interactivity, for example an electronic bulletin board?

- Do we want to provide an archive of past posts? If so, how should users be able to access the archive? How often will the archive be updated (daily, weekly, monthly)?

- Do we want to provide a site search engine?

- Do we want to provide a digest by e-mail to those who register?

- Do we want to be able to provide notification of updates to those who register?

- Do we want to provide an RSS feed?

Doug Goans and Teri M. Vogel, in an article that draws on their own experience of developing a library weblog system at Georgia State University (USA), say, 'We suggest that librarians who are considering blogging balance their goals with their available resources and personnel. The more technical support you have in-house or at your disposal, the more advanced system you can implement.'[1] Nevertheless, setting up the technology is just the beginning. A weblog implies a commitment to provide content on a regular basis over a long period of time. Chapter 7 will deal with the ongoing management issues involved in having a library weblog.

For those who are new to blogging, the best way to begin is to try a few of the free services by setting up a test weblog and defining its features. Not only will this help to give an idea of what is involved in creating and maintaining a weblog, but it will also help in understanding how weblog software works, how the updates are loaded to the server and the level of skills needed at each stage of the process. In addition, this experience will help in making decisions about weblog software and about weblog hosting. One of the advantages of using these web-based tools is that they are accessible from any computer that is linked to the Internet; a weblog can be updated from almost anywhere. 'By separating the content from the design, weblog tools give you a level of control and flexibility that would otherwise require a much higher level of technical savvy'.[2]

The free, web-based services are, in fact, where most people start. They all work in similar ways. The potential weblog owner registers on the website of the service and is allocated a username and password. The weblog owner then uses a web-based form on the website of the service to set up a weblog by first naming it, then specifying where the weblog will be hosted, then selecting a template to define how the pages of the weblog will look. The same form, or another, is used to specify the basic features of the weblog. After the weblog has been set up, the text of each post is typed into another form on the website of the weblog service; this creates a new file and allocates a filename to it. One click and the new post is uploaded to the weblog, whether on a hosting service provided by the weblog service or on the blogger's own server. The date and time stamp is added to the post automatically; the name and/or e-mail address of the poster may also be added (some services allow the weblog owner to make this decision). The new post will appear at the top of the current page of the weblog and older posts will gradually move down the page (as each new post is added) until they are archived (if an archive has been set up as one of the basic features of the weblog).

This makes weblog creation and management sound simple and, indeed, at the basic level it is. However, to take any weblog beyond the basics, some knowledge of HTML is needed; with some weblog software, a basic knowledge of HTML will be needed even to set up an archive. Moving beyond the free, web-based services, things become much more complex. The high-end systems may require a knowledge of Perl or CGI or other scripts. The software packages that people purchase to run on their own machines often work quite differently from each other and from the free, web-based services; weblog systems developed within an organisation may be even more different from each other and from the web-based services.

Any decision about weblog software need not necessarily be the 'final solution'. It is possible to migrate a weblog from one weblog software/system to another, particularly if the weblog owner has kept a backup of the archives. In an article written for his own *Library Stuff* weblog, Steven M. Cohen has described a series of moves, from Blogger to Movable Type to Radio and back to Blogger again.[3] These moves in no way reflect the quality of the software packages but rather a need to have support for particular weblog features and for particular versions of RSS. By the same token, any decision about weblog hosting also need not be final; it is, in fact, easier to move a weblog to a new host than to move it to new software. However, it is even easier if no changes have to be made to software or to hosting for the weblog.

Resources

DMOZ Open Directory Project: Weblogs: Tools

http://dmoz.org/Computers/Internet/On_the_Web/Weblogs/Tools/

Eatonweb Portal: Resources

http://portal.eatonweb.com/wlm/cat/tools

Weblog Compendium (Peter Scott)

http://www.lights.com/weblogs/tools.html

Weblog Hosting (Peter Scott)

http://www.lights.com/weblogs/hosting.html

Weblog Madness (no longer being updated)

http://www.larkfarm.com/weblog_madness.htm

Yahoo! Directories: Weblog Software

http://dir.yahoo.com/Computers_and_Internet/Internet/World_Wide_Web/Weblogs/Software/

Free weblog software options

Blogger was one of the first tools for weblog creation; as Neil McIntosh has said, it made 'the act of blogging much simpler by automating many of the most time-consuming and difficult stages of publishing'[4] a weblog. It still the best known of the free, web-based services; bought by Google in 2003, it has retained its popularity with users. Among those users are libraries, as indicated by the results of the research study reported in Chapter 5: Blogger was used as the basis for more library weblogs than any other weblog software option – more than two libraries in every five that had weblogs were using Blogger. The number of users has ensured that Blogger has been discussed in a number of magazine and journal articles and also widely reviewed.[5] However, there are other free weblog creation options, some of which are described below. Others can be located through the Internet directories and resources listed above.

Blog-City

http://www.blog-city.com/

The Blog-City home page claims that it 'offers one of the easiest ways to start blogging'. It is a web-based program that has a free version and a 'premium' version. The free version provides for comments, an online HTML editor, time and time zone 'stamping' of posts, archiving and an RSS feed, but it carries advertising. The premium version has no advertising. Additional features in the premium version include a photo album, statistics, visitor polls and domain naming. Weblog hosting is provided, with the URL in the form of 'http://weblogname.blog-city.com/'. The Blog-City website has a list of 'hot blogs', a 'random blog' button and a support weblog.

Blogger

http://www.blogger.com/

Blogger is a web-based service from Pyra Labs. Because the Blogger software runs on a central web server, users do not need to have special software on their own computer to use it, just a web browser. There are free and paid versions (the latter known as Blogger Pro). Blogger also provides hosting options through its Blog*Spot service. One result of the purchase by Google (the search engine) is that convenient access to Blogger is now provided as an option through the Google toolbar. Users of Blogger can create a weblog post that points to a web page they are visiting, and click 'Blog This!' on the toolbar – and their weblog will be updated.

Blosxom

http://www.blosxom.com/

'The zen of blogging', says the home page of Blosxom. This is a simple weblog system based on Perl; it can run on any system that supports Perl. Blosxom is downloaded to the user's own machine; some knowledge of the Internet and web servers is needed, and some set-up work is involved (particularly if Perl has to be installed first). Weblog posts are written using 'your favourite text editor', for example BBEdit (Macintosh), emacs (UNIX) or Notepad (Windows). Multiple weblogs can be created. There are customisable page templates and facilities are provided for permalinks and an archive. Documentation is available on the Blosxom website.

DiaryLand

http://www.Diaryland.com/

'Get your own fun, easy online diary!' says the DiaryLand home page. This is a free, web-based service. It provides page templates from among which choices can be made (the weblog owner can, however, also make changes by writing HTML). An archive can be created and there is an online guestbook. The weblog can be password protected to keep it private; if this is done, then the only people who can read the weblog are people to whom the weblog owner gives the password. A weblog URL will be in the form of 'http://weblogname.diaryland.com/'.

Greymatter

http://www.noahgrey.com/greysoft/

This weblog/journal writing software is available free for downloading from the Greymatter website, though 'donations are appreciated'. There is no advertising on weblogs created with Greymatter. The software provides for comments, site searching, FTP uploads to the weblog, image handling and support for 'multiple authors' (a collaborative weblog). User support is available through the Greymatter online discussion forum.

LiveJournal

http://www.livejournal.com/

This self-confessed 'simple to use blogging tool' is free. It can be used as a web-based service: users can maintain their weblog on the LiveJournal site. Alternatively, they can download the software (available for Windows, Macintosh, UNIX, BeOS). A paid version is also available. Bloggers can modify the appearance of their weblog through the use of templates, or they can use a 'customization wizard', or, for even tighter control, they can program the appearance of the weblog using the S2 programming language. Other scripting options provide for more functionality; for example, a Perl script enables bloggers to display the weblog on their own local website. An RSS feed can be developed, and a built-in aggregator allows bloggers to show feeds from other blogs as part of their weblog. Support is 'self-managed by volunteers'.

moTime

http://www.motime.com/

moTime promises 'instant publishing and communication'; the home page claims, 'You'll be online in less than five minutes'. The service is free, but a subscription is required for additional services such as an online photo gallery and domain name management/hosting. The website says that a moTime Pro service will soon be available for a fee. This web-based service (with weblog hosting) provides users with a recognisable URL, for example, *http://liverpoolliberalparty.motime.com/*. A user manual is available on the moTime website. A list of 'newly updated' blogs created with the software is also available through the moTime home page.

Pitas

http://www.pitas.com/

Pitas is a free, web-based service with weblog hosting. There is a selection of default page design templates, but it is possible to create a customised 'look and feel'. The system can be used to create a collaborative weblog – other people can be given posting rights. The home page has a list of 'most recent' weblogs created by members. A weblog URL will be in the form of '/http://weblogname.pitas.com/'.

Slash

http://www.slashcode.com/

This freeware can be downloaded from the Slash website. Slash is the source code for the well-known *Slashdot* weblog at *http://slashdot.org/*. With Perl capabilities, Slash has a number of advanced features but users will need technical knowledge and skills.

tBlog

http://www.tblog.com/

A web-based free service, tBlog claims that users can 'pick from our blog templates, customize a theme, and start blogging'. Weblog hosting is available for a small fee, and users of the Pro service get more features. There are no banner ads on the weblogs. Features include archiving of posts, comments, page visit statistics and image uploading. Users can add customisation by writing their own HTML code. The URL of a weblog hosted on the service will be in the recognisable form of 'http://weblogname.tblog.com/'. The tBlog home page provides lists of new weblogs created on the service, and a list of 'featured blogs'.

Tripod Blog Builder

http://blog.tripod.lycos.com/

A free, web-based service with ads on the pages. Tripod Plus, Tripod Pro and other paid membership options are available, and weblogs created through these options do not carry banner ads. Users can create and edit a weblog via the Tripod Blog Builder tools on the Tripod website. This allows for some customisation; in addition, HTML can be used for customisation of the weblog. The service includes website hosting and domain name registration. A JavaScript Library provides scripts for such features as a guestbook and user polls. There is an Image Gallery of free images for use on a weblog. The home page also provides access to tutorials, a list of 'most recently updated' weblogs and a 'blog directory' organised by broad subject.

Commercial weblog software options

Generally speaking, the paid weblog software options provide the weblog owner with more control than the free options, though there are exceptions. Troubleshooting can be done locally if the software is on the weblog owner's machine, whereas if a free, web-based service goes down, there is not much that the weblog owner can do about it. Some of the free weblog systems listed above also have paid (or commercial) versions. When this is the case, the paid version is free of advertisements. In addition, the paid versions usually have more features than the free versions. As with the free weblog systems, the commercial systems listed below vary a great deal in what they offer and how their features are implemented. The prices also vary, as does the type of support provided to users.

Blogger Pro

http://www.blogger.com/

- For an annual fee, Blogger Pro provides additional features over and above those that come with the free service (see above). However, in March 2004, the Blogger website was not accepting new orders for Blogger Pro because the software was being 'retooled'. Nevertheless, priority support was still being provided to Blogger Pro users.

Business Blogs: The B-Blog

http://www.n-ary.com/blogs/business.cfm

From Blog-City (see above), this is a commercial service for small to medium-size enterprises. A seven-day free trial is available. Weblog pages can be customised. Features include facilities for creating forms, image uploading, user polls, usage statistics and archiving. Weblog hosting is provided; weblog owners can use their own domain name.

Manila – Userland

http://manila.userland.com/

Manila from Userland is a more advanced system than their Radio (see below). Manila is described as a content management system for 'web publishing, weblog and collaboration tools for organizations'. Users can manage and syndicate (RSS) website content, build weblogs, create discussion groups, and create and manage e-mail update bulletins and newsletters. A 60-day trial copy of the software can be downloaded; an annual subscription is required for a licence for continued use. Subscribers are entitled to all system updates and feature enhancements. Some technical knowledge of the Internet and web servers is required to set up the system on a local machine. Academic pricing is available for 'qualified academic users' (see the Manila website for details). E-mail support is provided, and there is an online discussion group for users.

Movable Type

http://www.movable.org/

Users download the Movable Type software to their own machine. Commercial users pay a licence fee; from non-commercial users, a donation is requested. For a donation of US$20 or more, the weblog will appear on the 'recently updated' list on the Movable Type home page, and information will be provided about new software releases. Movable Type has facilities for 'template based customisation', comments, a site search engine, collaboration (multiple posters), an archive, image uploading and an RSS feed, and there is support for the creation of multiple weblogs. It is possible to ban nuisance commenters by IP address. Some knowledge of the Internet and web servers is needed; some local set-up work is also involved.

Onclave

http://www.onclave.com/

The Onclave weblog system is part of a suite of business software: 'Onclave solutions integrate information management tools with the collaborative timeliness of weblogging technology', says the home page. Onclave 'gives public relations agencies a powerful way to share and organize information internally and with clients'. The suite can be implemented as a knowledge management application to capture knowledge within the organisation in a naturalistic way. Interested people can request a trial through the Onclave website.

Radio – Userland

http://radio.userland.com/

Radio can be downloaded for a 30-day free trial; an annual fee is required for ongoing use. Weblog hosting is available. Radio is advertised as being 'suitable for personal or business users'. It is available in versions for Windows and Macintosh. An RSS feed is built in. Userland provides customer support by e-mail, and there is a discussion forum for users. The Radio home page has useful information, including a user guide.

TypePad

http://www.typepad.com/

TypePad is a simple 'hosted weblogging service' based on Movable Type. Because it is web-based, weblogs can be updated from any place where there is web access. Public or private (password protected) weblogs can be created. An online photo album can be incorporated, and a list of 'favourites' (a 'blogroll') can be maintained. Page design can be customised. There are various paid plans, including Basic, Plus and Pro; all have different features and facilities. The TypePad home page has a list of recently updated weblogs and 'featured blogs'. Moblogging facilities are 'coming soon'.

'Roll your own'

There are many reasons why an individual or a library might want to develop a weblog system in-house. If the weblog is to be database driven (for example, if it is to include regular updates from the library catalogue so that readers know what new books are in the library), then it would be possible to use a scripting language to create the weblog entries automatically whenever there are updates to the underlying database. Some database software (such as DB Textworks) has a web interface that could be used to create a weblog. In addition, some library automation systems have flexible web interfaces that could be adapted by someone with the technical expertise to serve the same purpose; it is possible that some automated library systems will provide for library weblogs in future versions. Some people have developed their own systems (whether database driven or not) in order to have greater control over features such as archiving or over the appearance of the weblog. Some weblogs, developed before the first specialist weblog software was released in 1999, were of necessity 'home-grown'. Finally, for some people, the challenge of writing their own code is half the fun of blogging.

Two examples from the professional literature will show why some organisations are making the decision to develop a weblog system in-house and how they have gone about the process of creating a weblog system. One was developed by an academic library in the United States; the other by an information service in the United Kingdom. In both cases, the people involved set out first to learn as much as they could about weblogs through practical experience as well as reading, and then made decisions about the kind of weblog that would best meet the needs of their organisation, taking into account the resources available for a weblog project.

Doug Goans and Teri M. Vogel, in their article mentioned earlier in this chapter, described the development of an in-house weblog system at their American university library, after a 'let's build it' decision had been made. They wanted to have 'absolute control over the features and functionality'; they wanted to 'incorporate the blog project into routine web database development endeavors' in the library; they wanted to be able to 'use the MySQL database already running' on-site to hold the weblog content; and they wanted to have a number of weblogs 'under a single administrative system'.[6] Four people were on the project's development team. A programmer worked with the team to design Active Server Pages (.asp) templates for the weblog and the interface to the MySQL database that powers the weblogs. The people who update the weblog are able to use a password-protected web-based form to manage database content; this provides a simple interface to the weblog system, and one that can be used from any computer linked to the Internet. Users, on the other hand, see quite a different view, with search and browse facilities and a link back to the library home page. Ongoing evaluation suggests that the system is 'working well to automate ... news'[7] and as a way 'to deliver timely and relevant news' to library patrons.

In a paper presented at the 'Online Information 2003' conference in London, Paul Squires described the development of *The Opportunity Wales Weblog*. Although not a library weblog as such, this is most definitely an information agency weblog. It comes from an organisation (Opportunity Wales) one of whose functions is to provide information about and support for e-commerce to small and medium-sized enterprises in the Objective One area of Wales.[8] Among other things, Opportunity Wales was influenced by coverage of weblogs in British newspapers like the *Guardian*. After experimenting with free and commercial weblog software, it was decided that a more complex content management system was needed for an Opportunity Wales weblog. The Opportunity Wales website was powered by the Obtree C4 content management suite, which had been used to develop services such as an e-mail newsletter in conjunction with the website. Paul Squires describes the decision-making process that led to the development of a community-based weblog that is an integral part of the Obtree work but which allows users to post messages and to search weblog content as a discrete collection of information separate from the other information provided by Opportunity Wales. The weblog, launched during Business Week in 2003, attracts around 50 posts each month and is the 'second most visited' area on the Opportunity Wales website.[9]

Weblog hosting: free services

Just as there are a number of options for weblog creation and maintenance, so there are a number of options for weblog hosting. In this section, some of the free weblog hosting services are described. Some of the free services also offer a for-fee option, usually with more features or without the advertisements that appear on many weblogs hosted on free services.

Blog*Spot

http://www.blogspot.com/

Blog*Spot is the free weblog hosting component of Blogger. One of the advantages of this service is that, in common with other free hosting services, it allows people who have no web server of their own to publish a weblog. Another advantage of Blog*Spot is that it provides several commercial upgrade options, so that bloggers can provide more sophisticated services as they gain more experience. For example, one of the upgrade options, Blog*Spot Plus, provides (for a small monthly fee) image hosting, usage statistics tracking, password protection (for private weblogs) and the possibility of multiple weblogs on one site.

In addition, the commercial (paid) services have no ads. An online tutorial is available.

Blogue

http://www.blogue.com/

Blogue is a hosting service for Manila-based weblogs. Further information was not available in March 2004, but Blogue is listed in a number of online directories.

Pitas

http://www.pitas.com/

Pitas provides free hosting for weblogs created using the Pitas web-based system. All that is required is that the weblog owner register on the Pitas website. The URL of the weblog will be in the form of 'http://username.pitas.com/' (see Pitas above under the free weblog software heading).

A number of other web-based weblog systems, like Pitas, provide free hosting for weblogs created using their system; these systems include Blog-City, Blosxom, DiaryLand and LiveJournal.

Peter Scott provides a long list of free and paid weblog hosting services on his *Weblog Compendium: Blog Hosting* page.[10] This list is international in scope, with services listed from the United States, the United Kingdom and New Zealand, among other countries. Some of the services listed are specifically for users of particular weblog systems, for example Blogger or Manila.

Weblog hosting: commercial services

Of the two examples of weblogs created by organisations that 'rolled their own' (above), one, Opportunity Wales, was using an external hosting service, while the other, Georgia State University Library, was using its own web server. In most communities today, there will be ISPs who provide web hosting services. Not all can support a weblog, but most can. Lists of ISPs can be found in the local 'yellow pages' telephone directory and in directories (including web-based directories) of local businesses.

For libraries that are creating a weblog, it would make sense to use the web hosting service of the library's own ISP, if the library already has a website, so that the library is dealing only with one external service provider for web and e-mail services. This will also ensure that both the library weblog and the library website have the same base URL. Assuming that the library already has a website, the other advantages of using the library's own web server, as outlined below, will also apply. If the library does intend to have its existing ISP host the weblog, then it will be necessary to choose a weblog management system that is compatible with the ISP's systems.

However, it is possible that a library might be exploring weblogs as a way of establishing a web presence for the first time, in which case the library would also be exploring web hosting for the first time. If this is the case, it is important that the library select an ISP that can handle weblogs created through its chosen weblog mangement system. Some commercial weblog hosts actually advertise themselves as being able to host weblogs created with Movable Type or Blogger or other weblog systems. The ISP will provide instructions (sometimes by e-mail, sometimes on paper, sometimes on a website) for uploading weblog updates via

FTP (File Transfer Protocol). These instructions must be followed exactly – the instructions will differ slightly from ISP to ISP.

Weblog hosting: the library's own web server

If the organisation already has a web server to host its own website, then it makes sense to use this server for hosting a weblog too – unless there is a technical reason why the server cannot accommodate a weblog. The server will already be in place and the set-up will have been done. The organisation will have complete control of the server. Support will be available. The library staff will not be dealing with one service provider for website hosting and another for weblog hosting. The weblog and the website will both have the same base URL. It will be easier to give the same 'look and feel' to the weblog pages as to the pages on the library website, using the same basic page layout, graphics, colours and typography on both. In addition, it will be easier to have additional pages that are not typically provided with specialised weblog software on a weblog hosting service – for example, an 'about us' page.

Moblogging

Photoblogs and moblogs help people and organisations to create and maintain a record of what they are doing – whether it be a family on holiday, or a group of people working on a project, or a community activity organised by a library, or one of any number of possible applications. While many ISPs can provide hosting facilities for moblogs, not all are able to do so. As a result, specialist moblog hosting services have emerged. For example, the textamerica[11] service enables users to post pictures, video and text from a camera phone. It is a free service; online registration is available. There are links on the textamerica home page to selected moblogs hosted on the site and technical information is provided. A Google[12] search using the terms 'moblog' and 'hosting' will return a long list of free and paid moblog hosting options.

New tools for moblogging are emerging all the time. Whether or not these tools are appropriate for library applications remains to be seen. It may be, though, that libraries are more limited by imagination than any other factor when looking at these tools. While this book was being prepared, Nokia, the Finnish and international mobile phone leader, announced the development of Lifeblog PC software that will enable users of Nokia's camera phones to create weblogs from their phone.[13] This software will enable users to bring together and organise information in various ways, including on a timeline. Users will be able to incorporate still and video images, e-mail messages and text from a word processor, among other resources, into their own biographical blog. The Lifeblog software on the personal computer, when the mobile phone is connected to the machine, downloads all the material that is stored on the phone; images, sound and text from other sources can also be added. A cut-down version of Lifeblog on the mobile phone handset will enable people to see how the content they are capturing will be arranged. This technology may enable libraries to create newsletters, record community events and collect local history information, among other applications.

RSS feeds

RSS is a widely-accepted format for sharing or syndicating content on the Web, including via weblogs. There are some people who believe that 'RSS is not ready for prime time',[14] and there are even people who use RSS who share their concerns about RSS.[15] Nevertheless, at the moment it is the best tool we have for the purpose, and many people are making use of its features. There are a number of benefits to providing an RSS feed on a library weblog – benefits to the library and to the users. These benefits include the following:

- The RSS feed allows potential users to see a summary of the content of the library weblog without actually visiting it; if they find the summary appealing then they are likely to click through to the weblog.

- The content of the library weblog will be picked up by more search engines (particularly the specialist weblog and RSS feed search engines) and directories; it will also be picked up more easily by other weblogs. This means that the content of the library weblog will be distributed more widely and be seen by more people.

- Some other libraries in the community may pick up the RSS feed on their website and make the information available to their users, too.

- Regular users of the library weblog will be able to read updates through an RSS feed reader or aggregator, along with the updates to all the other weblogs that they monitor. If the content of the library weblog is made available to the user in this way, and the user does not have to make a special visit to the library's weblog 'just in case there is an update', then the user may be more prepared to continue to monitor the weblog.

- The provision of an RSS feed is an indication of a professional approach to information service via a weblog.

If one of the aims of a library weblog is publicity and promotion for the library and its services, then RSS will help to
assist this aim by bringing users to the weblog directly or
through an aggregator.

RSS is an XML (eXtensible Markup Language) format,
not the simple HTML that is the basis of many web pages.
This means that additional software is required to read the
content of the RSS files on a web page. This might be via a
web-based aggregator, or via a program that is downloaded
to the user's own computer. What an RSS feed actually
looks like in XML will depend on the version of RSS that is
being used – it is human readable but not easily so. The RSS
feed can be written 'by hand' with a simple text editor.
Alternatively, it can be generated automatically by some of
the weblog creation software (such as Manila and Movable
Type), by a database using a scripting language such as Perl
or PHP, by some content management programs or by
specialist tools such as *RSS Master 1.0*[16] (which is available
free). The following document, available on the World Wide
Web, provides a good introduction for people who plan to
add an RSS feed to a weblog:

RSS – A Primer for Publishers and Content Providers

http://www.eevl.ac.uk/rss_primer/

The Introduction states that the purpose of this document is
to explain the basic concepts behind RSS and to answer
some frequently asked questions. 'It is primarily intended
for a non-technical audience who require an overview of
RSS in order to allow them to make decisions regarding the
possible use of the technology'. The document also provides
'recommendations for good practice, case studies on RSS

production and links to tools and specifications which will provide useful starting points'.

One of the problems associated with RSS at present is that there are different versions of RSS and they are not necessarily compatible. RSS 1.0 is probably the most commonly used format, but others such as 0.9 and 2.0 also have their advocates.[17] In choosing weblog creation software, the library may also be choosing an RSS format; the same is true when choosing a weblog hosting service. For libraries, the most important thing is that the people who create the library weblog are aware of the options available to them. For example, selecting an RSS validator depends on knowing what RSS format is being used. However, apart from making sure that decisions taken at any one time do not reduce the options available later, the advice from Jason Cook on *Webmonkey* is 'not to dwell on these details when you're getting started'.[18]

The RSS feed will be used across a wide range of aggregators and the content should appear without errors in any setting. To ensure this, it is important that the XML be validated before it is used on the weblog. There are a number of RSS validators on the Web that allow bloggers and others to check their RSS feeds. Among these validators are the following:

Redland RSS 1.0 Validator and Viewer (David Beckett)

http://www.redland.opensource.ac.uk/rss/

RSS Validator for 2.0 and other versions (Mark Pilgrim and Sam Ruby)

http://feeds.archive.org/validator/

Once the RSS feed has been validated, it can be added to the weblog. It is considered courteous to include a visual indication that a weblog has an RSS feed; this is often done by putting a small XML or RSS or RDF icon on the main page of the weblog. Alternatively, there may be a link labelled 'Syndicate this site'.

Additional features

The potential for adding features to a weblog does not end with RSS. A post on a Canadian weblog called *The Blog Driver's Waltz* advises:

> Don't think of a blog ... as a flat item, or one that stands alone without consideration of the other pieces. Blogs can incorporate oodles of other components, modules or whatever else you might like to call them. Bulletin boards, calendars, document archives, FAQs, downloads, RSS feeds, RSS aggregation within your web page ... you name it, it can probably get spliced in somewhere.[19]

Searchable databases linked to the weblog, audio and video features – these are already possible. Weblogs are very much a developing tool; it will be possible to add even more features in the future.

This chapter has dealt with weblog creation; Chapter 7 will cover planning for the development of a library weblog and ongoing weblog maintenance and management.

References

1. Doug Goans and Teri M. Vogel, 'Building a Home for Library News With a Blog', *Computers in Libraries* 23.10 (2003): 25.

2. Joshua Allen, 'The Weblog Tool Roundup', *Webmonkey* 2 May 2002, online (available at *http://hotwired.lycos.com/webmonkey/02/18/index3a.html?w=eg20020503* accessed 4 May 2002).

3. Steven M. Cohen, 'From MT to Radio to Blogger – A Journey', *Library Stuff* [weblog] 6 Jan. 2004, online (available at *http://radio.weblogs.com/0124132/stories/2004/01/06/fromMtToRadioToBloggerAJourny.html* accessed 8 Jan. 2004).

4. Neil McIntosh, 'A Tale of One Man and His Blog', *Guardian* 31 Jan. 2002, online (available at *http://www.guardian.co.uk/online/story/0,3605,641742,00.html* accessed 15 Apr. 2002).

5. See, for example, Biz Stone, 'Labs, Robots, and Giant Floating Brains: The Amazingly True Story of Blogger!', *Webreview* 9 Mar. 2001, online (available at *http://www.webreview.com/2001/03-09/strategists/index02.shtml* accessed 16 Mar. 2002).

6. Doug Goans and Teri M. Vogel, 'Building a Home for Library News With a Blog', *Computers in Libraries* 23.10 (2003): 24.

7. Doug Goans and Teri M. Vogel, 'Building a Home for Library News With a Blog', *Computers in Libraries* 23.10 (2003): 26.

8. *http://www.opportunitywales.co.uk/*

9. Paul Squires, 'The Opportunity Wales Weblog', *Online Information 2003 Proceedings, 2–4 December 2003, London, UK*, eds Catherine Graham, Jonathan Lewis and Alison Yates (Oxford: Learned Information, 2003).

10. *http://www.lights.com/weblogs/hosting.html*

11. *http://www.textamerica.com/*

12. *http://www.google.com/*

13. Mark Ward, 'Log Your Life via Your Phone', *BBC News* 10 Mar. 2004, online (available at *http://news.bbc.co.uk/1/hi/technology/3497596.stm* accessed 15 Mar. 2004).

14. See, for example, Dylan Greene, '10 Reasons Why RSS Is Not Ready for Prime Time', *Dylan Greene dot com* [weblog]

21 Jan. 2004, online (available at *http://www.dylangreene.com/blog.asp?blogID=363* accessed 3 Feb. 2004).

15. Walt Crawford, 'The Great RSS Debate', *Cites & Insights* 3.12 (2003): 3–4.

16. *http://www.softtool.info/RSSMaster/*

17. Paul Festa, 'Battle of the Blog: Dispute Exposes Bitter Power Struggle Behind Web Logs', *CNETNews.com* 4 Aug. 2003, online (available at *http://news.com.com/2009-1032-5059006.html?part=dht&tag=ntop* accessed 28 Aug. 2003).

18. Jason Cook, 'Sharing Your Site With RSS', *Webmonkey* 14 May 2003, online (available at *http://hotwired.lycos.com/webmonkey/03/17/index3a.html* accessed 15 May 2003).

19. 'Why RSS? Why Blogs? Why? Why? Why?', *The Blog Driver's Waltz* [weblog] 15 Apr. 2003, online (available at *http://www.blogdriverswaltz.com/archive/000241.html#000241* accessed 18 Apr. 2003).

7

Managing the library weblog

Library weblogs can serve a number of purposes; this is clear from the professional literature reviewed in Chapter 5. Among other things, it has been suggested that library weblogs can be used to provide current information for library users, to assist library staff and users to locate relevant resources on the Internet, and to promote the library and its services. Indeed the study of library weblogs carried out in October and November 2003 shows that some libraries are using weblogs in these ways. However, not all the purposes that have been suggested for library weblogs are appropriate for every library. Each library will need to make its own decision about whether or not to have a library weblog and what purpose or purposes that library weblog will be designed to serve, and then develop the weblog accordingly.

The library weblog: an overview of the management issues

Websites and weblogs are not always developed or managed in such a way that they help libraries to achieve their mission or goals. Resources of time, skills, money and computing power are needed for a library weblog. Just as with any other project, the resources devoted to a library weblog should further the aims of the library. A strategic planning approach to the creation, development and maintenance of a library weblog will assist in the management process. Strategic planning relates the activities of an organisation such as a library to the mission and goals that should guide the activities of the organisation, provides a basis for the allocation of resources to a project and provides a framework for its evaluation. The strategic planning process as it might be applied to a library weblog is summarised in Figure 7.1.[1]

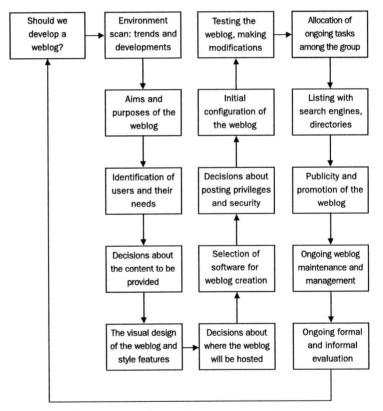

Figure 7.1 The strategic planning/development cycle as applied to a library weblog

The strength of this approach is that it covers the weblog development and management process from the time that the original planning question is asked – 'Should we have a library weblog?' – through all the planning phases from the establishment of the weblog to its ongoing operation and evaluation, and relates it to the cycles of other aspects of an organisation's planning. It also provides a basis for the consideration of issues that are important at each stage of the process. These issues include identification of potential users and their needs, selection and presentation of content, navigational aids for users of the weblog, value-added information services provided via the weblog, and the ongoing monitoring and evaluation of the weblog.

The strategic planning process provides a basis for the identification of the resources and skills that will be needed at each stage of the weblog planning and development process. The following resources may be needed at any or all stages of the process, depending on the nature of the weblog:

- personnel/skills;
- time;
- money;
- facilities, software tools, equipment.

Of these, the most important is people (and their skills). The strategic planning process helps library managers to identify the skills that will be needed at all stages of the planning and development process and the skills that will be needed at only one or two stages. Figure 7.1 suggests that the following skills, among others, are needed at various stages in the process of creating and managing a library weblog:

- management and planning skills;

- writing and/or journalism skills;

- editing skills;

- skills of information evaluation, analysis, organisation and presentation;

- visual, photographic and/or graphic design skills;

- Internet search skills;

- HTML and other web development language/scripting skills;

- skills in using particular weblog software packages (and any necessary related skills – for example, if the software requires a knowledge of a scripting language or of a database system);

- skills in maintaining a web server;

- public relations skills;

- interpersonal skills.

It may be that some of these skills are available in-house (in the library or elsewhere in the organisation of which the library is a part), while for some others the library might rely on an ISP (Internet service provider) or an outside consultant. Any or all of these aspects of weblog development might be contracted to other parties, in which case project oversight and management skills will be necessary within the library or information agency so that the weblog continues to meet the organisation's goals.

There may be considerable differences in the requirements for an 'ordinary' library website and for a library weblog. For example, in the case of a library website, it is probable that there will be a need for writing skills and editing skills at the stage when the basic web pages are being created, but once the site is in operation, the need for these skills will decrease – particularly if the site will be relatively stable over time. With a weblog, on the other hand, the need for writing and editing skills will be ongoing and will not decrease with time. Without the ongoing allocation of time and resources for weblog content, the weblog will cease to attract a readership.

In this chapter, each of the aspects of the weblog planning and development process as outlined in Figure 7.1 will be discussed, but under broader headings. Although the planning process may commence at any stage of the cycle, this chapter will follow the sequence from the initial decision to establish a weblog, through all the various phases, to evaluation. Evaluation should feed back into the cycle, helping library staff to make decisions about whether or not the library project is worthwhile and whether or not it should continue. Some of the stages of the strategic planning process will be undertaken simultaneously, and perhaps by different people. What is important is that all the stages of the process do occur and that they feed into each other. A library weblog represents an investment of time and money, and planning will help to ensure that the library benefits from this investment.

Planning for the implementation of a library weblog

The strategic planning process begins with the answer to the question, 'Should the library have a weblog?' If the answer is 'What's a weblog?' then some professional development activity will be needed before a sensible decision can be made. If the answer is 'Yes', then the next question becomes 'What kind of weblog should we have?'

The next step is an 'environment scan': an investigation of current trends and developments in weblogs in general and in library weblogs in particular. What other libraries have created weblogs? How are other libraries using their weblogs? How successful have those weblogs been? The research study reported in Chapter 5 will help to answer these questions. The environment scan should also cover the software and hardware currently available for weblog creation and hosting (see Chapter 6) and the resources that the library has available to it for weblog development.

The mission statement, aims and objectives or goals of a library should provide the basis for developing the aims and objectives for a weblog. An analysis of the mission statement of the library (if one exists), the service goals and objectives and any other relevant documentation will help to focus ideas about a weblog. Only half of the library weblogs that were studied in October and November 2003 incorporated any kind of statement about aims or purposes, and some of those statements were very brief and very informal. It is hard to imagine that many of the statements of purpose could have served as a basis for making decisions about the weblog. Other library weblogs appeared to have no real purpose, raising the question of why resources should have been devoted to them. When only a little over half even had a link back to the library's home page, it is hard to believe that they were acting as a public relations or marketing tool for the library. Why, then, were they being supported at all? Defining the broad aims and purposes of the weblog project within the context of the library's own mission and goals will help to focus the work on the weblog and to justify it.

It will help if, at this stage, the library begins to work on a weblog policy and guidelines. As decisions are made about the weblog, then the policy and guidelines can be revisited and revised as necessary. Some of the issues that should be addressed in the policy include responsibility for the weblog and its content, editorial control over content and frequency of updating.

Identifying the potential users of the library weblog

The specific goals for a library weblog will be developed from the broad aims and objectives. The needs of potential users of the weblog are important in defining the specific goals. The potential users of the weblog should be identified and their needs investigated. If the needs of the potential users are not clearly understood, then those needs cannot be met through a weblog.

Will the library weblog be aimed at all users of the library? If so, there are two important considerations here. First, will all library users have the knowledge, skills and access to technology that are needed to read a weblog and perhaps contribute to it? Secondly, unless the library users are a very homogeneous group (lawyers in a law firm, for example), then it is hard to imagine that one weblog might appeal to the interests of all library users. Users of a public library are usually very diverse in age, interests and tastes. Even in a school, the library users will usually include students of different ages and interests as well as their teachers. If the weblog is to be designed to meet the needs of a particular group of library users (for example, teenage users of a public library), then the needs and interests of those teens should help to guide the development of the weblog.

The usual advice to weblog developers is to ask people who represent the target audience for the weblog what they would like to have in a library weblog. Unfortunately, many people who might use a library weblog know too little about weblogs and their potential applications to be able to voice an opinion. Focus groups might help here, with participants being shown examples of weblogs and then asked for comments and ideas. Another approach might be to involve potential users of the weblog in the decision-making process, perhaps by inviting them to join an advisory committee. Most libraries will already have a good idea of the needs and interests of their users since this information is needed for collection development among other things. More of a problem is identifying the needs of those potential users of the weblog who are not users of the library. Investigating existing local weblogs and their readers or contributors may help here. In any case, if a library is planning to create a weblog, then library staff should be aware of other weblogs in their community, what they offer and the people who use them.

Another aspect of user needs that should be considered at this level of planning is the kind of Internet access that potential users of the weblog will have. If the library already has a website, then this information will already have been collected as part of the planning process for that project. If it was not collected at that stage, then the log files generated through usage of a library website (and normally available from the ISP) will provide some indication of numbers of users and where they are coming from. Some of the visit counters that are available for websites also provide statistics on the hardware and software that people are using to access the site. If the library does not already have a website, then a simple survey form, handed out and collected at the circulation desk or printed on a postcard and inserted into one of the books borrowed by each library user, could be used to collect basic information about Internet access and experience.

Making decisions about content and other features

Identification of potential users of a library weblog will help to determine the kind of information and facilities that will be provided through a library weblog. No weblog can be 'all things to all people'. It is probable (but by no means certain) that the potential users of a library's weblog will be very similar to the users of that library's information, resources and services 'in real life', though the geographical distribution of the users might change.

The following are possible sources of content for a library weblog; not all will be appropriate for every library weblog, depending on the aims or purposes of the weblog and the intended users.

- content created within the library, for example news items related to library activities, functions to be held in the library, new items in the library collection, media releases generated by the library, book reviews written by library staff;

- content available in library databases such as the library catalogue or any special databases created by the library;

- content and links selected from among the material available on the Internet;

- material available via RSS feeds from other sites or as streaming media (for example, a news ticker);

- content provided by readers of the weblog, for example through comments on posts. Other content provided by readers might include book reviews, local news items, information about Internet resources or other information relevant to the topic or theme or readership of the weblog.

It may be necessary for the library to include in the weblog policy or guidelines a statement about the content of the weblog. Certainly, decisions will have to be made about topic coverage of the weblog, how Internet resources will be selected and evaluated, what kinds of posts or comments are appropriate, quality standards, responsibility for the content and links, and any moderation of comments or posts from readers. Who will have final responsibility for content and standards? Will 'anything' be allowed or will someone make decisions about what will appear? What will be done about inappropriate material? The aims of the weblog and the needs of the intended audience will provide a basis for policy development and for ongoing decision-making about content.

Although it seems obvious, many organisations do not understand that writing for the Web, really is writing. Writing for a weblog is just as public as writing a print brochure. It requires good writing skills – not just a command of the rules of grammer and syntax, but the ability to present material in an interesting way. On the Web, people have access to millions of alternatives should the library weblog prove unappealing. There are a number of issues to be considered in relation to writing for the Web. Who are the likely users of the weblog? What level and type of language will appeal to them? Should the writing be formal or informal? Should the writing style on the library weblog be different from that on the library website and from that in the library's print publications? If the latter is the case, then material from the library's print publications and media releases will need to be rewritten for the weblog.

The information architecture of a weblog is as important as the content. The term 'information architecture' is used to describe the ways in which information can be organised and presented to meet the needs of the users. The basic information architecture of a weblog is defined by the standard weblog format of short posts arranged in chronological order with the most recent first. However, even given this common basic format, some weblogs are easier to use than others. On the Web, there are two main levels of information architecture, both of which apply to weblogs:

- the organisation of information on the site as a whole; and

- the organisation of information within the individual pages of a site.

On a weblog, information architecture incorporates developing a classification or structure for the site as a whole, specifiying the relationship of the pages of the site to each other and developing structures for organising content on the individual pages. While the weblog posts will be in reverse date order, what about the 'blogrolls', the lists of links to other weblogs or other Internet resources that are provided by many bloggers? Many bloggers just present lists, but others attempt to classify their links, though the classifications vary a great deal. The important thing, from the point of view of the reader, is that the classification make sense and leads the reader to sources that are interesting or helpful.

The navigation tools for users should help them to find information in the weblog by making the underlying information architecture transparent for them.[2] The navigation tools should help users to maintain a mental map of where they are in a website, they should make it clear how the various parts of the website relate to each other and they should be the basis of tools that help users to find specific items of information on the site. Tools for navigation of a weblog include:

- menus;

- directories and lists;

- navigation panels;

- buttons;

- a site map;

- a site search engine;

- colours (for background, headings or lettering);

- symbols.

Many sites employ a number of these tools or strategies so that users always have a number of visual clues to help them to orient themselves within the site and to find information.

The visual design of a weblog should, on the one hand, identify it as an activity of the library and, on the other and, be relevant to the needs and interests and tastes of users of the weblog and related to the subject matter of the weblog. It should also be in keeping with current trends in web design. The 'look and feel' of a weblog will be an important factor in attracting readers. The visual design of a weblog includes:

- the creation and use of images;

- logos and other graphics;

- photographs;

- typography;

- backgrounds;

- navigation panels and buttons;

- use of colour.

It may be worth hiring a graphic designer to work on the weblog pages, unless design skills are available in-house. A professionally designed logo or masthead will make a great deal of difference to the appearance and appeal of a weblog.

Establishing the weblog

In Chapter 6, the weblog software options and the weblog hosting options were discussed. To a certain extent, the software decision will depend on where the weblog is to be hosted. Table 6.1 provides a summary of the advantages and disadvantages of each of the four main software and hosting options. However, decisions about weblog software and hosting are not the only technical decisions to be made.

In terms of the weblog server or host, the main question to be resolved is whether or not the library will establish and maintain its own server, or whether it will use space on the web server of, for example, an ISP or the organisation of which the library is a part. If the library already has a website, then it is most likely that the weblog would be hosted on the same server as the website. No web space is really 'free'; there will be costs involved in any of the options even if there is no direct charge. Whatever the decision about weblog hosting, procedures may need to be established for posting official information.

Security is an important issue for weblogs, particularly related to interactivity. One of the central ideas of blogging is the creation of a 'community' around the weblog. While this is a strength, it also poses security problems. If more than one person in the library will post to the library weblog then, again, security is a concern. If a number of people will be able to post, then will one person have designated responsibility for content? If so, then that person may have to approve posts before they are 'published'; alternatively, that person may have a level of access sufficient to delete or amend posts once they are made. If all people who post have the same level of access, then all those people share final responsibility for content. If readers can initiate discussion by posting new messages to the weblog, will the library staff be able to amend or delete inappropriate posts? If readers can post comments on other posts, will the library staff be able to delete inappropriate comments or spam? What measures will be taken to deal with spam? What support does the weblog hosting service or ISP provide in relation to dealing with spam?

Testing of the weblog is an ongoing process, though it is particularly important when the weblog is first made available. The weblog site as a whole and the individual pages should be tested thoroughly at the beginning, and any necessary modifications made. However, testing needs to be ongoing. This testing should have a number of aspects:

- testing against the original aims/objectives and the needs of users;

- testing of features and links to make sure that they are operational;

- testing the weblog in as many different browsers as possible, and on as many different kinds of computers as possible, to ensure that the design and features work across different hardware and software configurations;

- testing any navigation tools on the weblog to make sure that they work properly and assist the users to explore the weblog and to locate information.

People who have not been involved in the design and development process should be involved in the testing process. These people should, as a group, resemble the potential user group/s for whom the weblog was designed.

Making decisions about and managing interactivity

If the library weblog is to be interactive, then someone on the library staff (or several people) should be given the responsibility of interacting with the users of the weblog. Even if interactivity is restricted to a 'clickable' contact e-mail address, someone on the library staff should be reading e-mail to that address several times a day, and either responding to messages or forwarding the messages to other people on the staff who can supply information or comment. The more sophisticated the interactivity, the more library staff time will be required. Comments from readers will need to be monitored. Someone on the library staff may need to facilitate and moderate discussion on an electronic bulletin board or discussion forum. Discussions happen because someone initiates them. Discussions can degenerate into 'flame wars' or stray off-topic unless someone is moderating them. A library patron may volunteer – but even in this case the responsibility for a library weblog still rests with the library.

Some weblogs handle discussion in a password-protected area. This is the case, for example, with the *Blogger Book Club* weblog of Roselle Public Library (USA).[3] This solves the problem of spam (though not necessarily the problem of inappropriate posts). However, setting up a password-protected area requires that usernames and passwords be allocated to authorised users, that a secure system be implemented, and that security be monitored. Someone has to answer questions about access to the secure area; someone has to deal with the problems of lost or forgotten passwords. In addition, as for an open, public system, discussions need to be monitored and moderated.

Ongoing maintenance and management

Although this stage is represented by just a couple of boxes in Figure 7.1, this is, in fact, the stage that covers most of the life of the weblog. This is the stage that requires the ongoing commitment from the library – this is where 'real life' takes place. The weblog has been developed and is operational. Management and maintenance procedures have been established. At this point, many libraries consider their work on the project to be completed: they have a weblog and now they can move on to other things. However, a weblog represents an ongoing activity. It has to be monitored and tended carefully, in the light of new developments in the library and in the environment in which the library operates, and in the light of new Internet trends and developments. The following, among others, are aspects of ongoing weblog development and maintenance that need to be considered and planned for:

- monitoring visits to the weblog and use of any special features;

- ongoing evaluation of the extent to which the weblog meets user needs;

- ongoing evaluation of the weblog in relation to new developments in information technology in general and the Internet and blogging in particular;

- regular updating of content;

- adding new services and features to the weblog;

- checking and maintaining links;

- maintaining navigational structures;

- checking listings of the weblog by search engines and directories to ensure that they remain current;

- responding to any e-mail and other correspondence related to the weblog;
- maintaining and updating the hardware and software that support the weblog;
- training of library staff and users;
- ongoing publicity and promotion of the weblog;
- planning for the future.

To achieve these things, resources, including staff time, will have to be allocated. Who will carry out the tasks? How will these people be supervised? The staff members involved will need to have appropriate skills. A budget will be needed.

Budgeting for the weblog

In budgeting for a library weblog, two types of costs should be considered: once-only costs associated with setting up the weblog; and ongoing costs that will continue as long as the library is involved in blogging. The costs will vary for each library, depending on the weblog options or paths selected for the library weblog and the extent to which the library is able to make use of free services or to have work undertaken by people in-house as part of their normal jobs. The following are once-only costs (at least until updates are necessary):

- purchase of any necessary software;
- purchase of any necessary hardware, including scanner, moblogging equipment;
- design of pages, graphics, logos.

The following are ongoing costs:

- annual licence fees for any necessary software;
- annual fees for weblog hosting (if necessary);
- staff time necessary for monitoring the weblog and responding to comments, e-mail messages and other queries;
- staff time necessary for publicity and promotion of the weblog;
- staff time necessary for creating weblog content;
- staff time necessary for supporting any interactivity;
- costs of continuing professional development activities for library staff (if necessary);
- costs of technical support;
- costs of maintaining any computer hardware and other equipment (for example, scanners and mobile phones to create content);
- costs associated with ongoing evaluation of the weblog.

Promoting the weblog

In order to capitalise on their investment in a weblog, libraries and information agencies should take steps to ensure that as many people as possible visit the weblog – and, in particular, that as many people in the target group as possible visit the weblog. There is little point in having a weblog if no one visits it. There is little point in providing a weblog if the potential users in the target group do not know about it. However, publicity and promotion have to be ongoing. It is not enough to promote the weblog when it first appears; new 'generations' of potential weblog readers are emerging all the time as skills and access to technology improve.

Having a weblog listed with appropriate directories and search engines is the first step in bringing the weblog to the attention of potential users. The general search engines like Google[4] and AlltheWeb[5] use crawlers to build their databases, but also welcome submissions (first check to make sure the weblog is not already listed!). Most of the search engines and directories add websites and weblogs to their databases in two ways: they send out 'spiders' or 'crawlers' or software robots to identify new websites; and they accept recommendations from website developers and users (usually on a web-based form). Bear in mind that some of the search engines take as long as three months or more to process information about a website and list it after information about it has been submitted on the form. All of the specialist weblog search engines and directories welcome submissions; see Chapter 3 for lists of these search engines and directories. There are also search engines and directories that cover particular topics, such as library and information science, or education, or literacy. Anyone who is developing a weblog should become familiar with the search engines and directories that cover the same subject matter as the weblog, as well as with the general search engines.

Other steps that library weblog owners can take to promote the weblog include the following (not all will be appropriate for every weblog):

- Disseminate media releases in print and e-mail form, and wherever possible target them to the particular media outlet.

- Ensure that all stationery used by the library or information agency, all business cards and all e-mail electronic signatures carry the URL of the library weblog.

- Create print materials that will advertise or promote the weblog – for example, small brochures, bookmarks, stickers, postcards.

- Ensure that the URL appears in any local information or trade directories.

- Link to the library weblog from the home page of the library website.

- Ensure that the library's parent organisation (university, school, local government authority, business, government agency, company) features the URL on their website.

- Write about the weblog in appropriate newsletters, professional journals and local and trade publications.

- Offer conference presentations, papers and poster sessions about the weblog to organisers of conferences and seminars, including local conferences and seminars in other professional or special-interest fields.

- Notify local service clubs and other local organisations and offer to make presentations at meetings.

- Notify local ISPs so that the weblog is listed in any directories that they might create.

- Make contacts within the local blogging community, link to local weblogs and request links in return.

- Post comments to relevant weblogs (including local weblogs) that contribute to discussion but also make reference to the library weblog.

- Have a small logo or button that other bloggers (and other websites) can download and use as a link to the library weblog.

- Take an Internet-enabled mobile phone or camera to local events and post to the weblog from the event, with links to sources of information (for some people, their first experience of a weblog has come when they have been 'blogged').

■ Nominate for any local and international weblog awards – these can help to generate publicity at the local level among potential users of the weblog.

Evaluating the weblog project

There are two kinds of evaluation that are relevant to a project such as a weblog: ongoing formative evaluation and summative evaluation (evaluation carried out at the point where project implementation might be said to have been completed). The two forms of evaluation serve different purposes. Formative evaluation feeds back into the project development cycle at all stages, providing information that will help the weblog owner to manage the weblog in such a way that it continues to reflect the aims and objectives of the organisation and to meet user needs. Summative evaluation, on the other hand, provides information for reporting on a project at critical stages of implementation and at the completion of the project. In as much as a weblog is never 'complete', formative evaluation is probably more important in this case, though funding authorities will want summative information from time to time.

Every weblog should be reviewed at regular intervals, perhaps at times when budget decisions are being made. At this time, attention should be paid to the following questions, among others:

■ Is the weblog still serving a useful purpose in terms of the aims, objectives, goals, user needs and the needs of the library?

- Does the weblog make appropriate use of newly emerging developments in Internet technology?

- Is the weblog fulfilling the aims that were established for it? Are those aims still appropriate?

- Who is actually using the weblog and why? Are they the people for whom the weblog was originally designed?

Information collected through this review process feeds through to the beginning of a new cycle in the strategic planning process for the weblog.

There are many different strategies and techniques that could be used for ongoing monitoring and evaluation of weblogs; however, not all will be appropriate or useful in all settings. These strategies and techniques include:

- questionnaire surveys (using mailed forms, online forms and/or forms distributed in the library);

- collecting information from participants in Internet courses and workshops organised by the library;

- focus groups representative of the various potential user groups of the library weblog;

- interviews (in person or by e-mail) with users of the library weblog or people who contribute comments to the weblog;

- if interactivity is a feature of the weblog, keeping a record of the number of comments or posts from users;

- monitoring references and links to the website on other weblogs (perhaps using web-based links tracers) and on RSS feeds;

- monitoring references to the weblog in local newspapers and newsletters and in the professional literature;

- technical tools and strategies, including counters and trackers on the weblog's main page, a guestbook on the weblog and link searches on the search engines;

- benchmarking against leading weblogs from other libraries and information services;

- formal evaluation of the weblog by an outside, independent expert or consultant.

The strategic planning process provides a useful framework within which to view the many tasks associated with weblog development and maintenance and to conceptualise their relationship to one another. It brings together information about the personnel (and skills), facilities and equipment, software, financial investment and time commitment that will be necessary at each stage of the weblog development process, matching them to the tasks that need to be undertaken at each stage. In this way, it facilitates forward planning for weblog development. It also highlights the reality that weblog development and maintenance are ongoing activities, not a 'one-off project'. Resources have to be allocated to the weblog on a continuing basis. Thus the strategic planning process can assist library management to plan appropriately for the creation and management of a library weblog within the context of the aims and goals of the library and the needs of its users.

References

1. This figure is adapted from one describing the library website development process in Laurel A. Clyde, 'A Strategic Planning Approach to Web Site Management', *The Electronic Library* 18.2 (2000): 97–108.

2. See, for example, J. Fleming, *Web Navigation: Designing the User Experience* (New York: O'Reilly, 1998); K.L. Garlock and S. Pionek, *Designing Web Interfaces to Library Services and Resources* (Chicago, IL: American Library Association, 1998); J. Nielsen, *Designing Web Usability: The Practice of Simplicity* (Indianapolis, IN: New Riders, 1999).

3. *http://www.roselle.lib.il.us/YouthServices/BookClub/ Bloggerbookclub.htm*

4. *http://www.google.com/*

5. *http://www.alltheweb.com/*

8

Sources of information about weblogs

This book provides an introduction to weblogs and blogging in a library and information science context. Further information about weblogs and blogging can be found in printed sources, in web-based sources and in a number of specialist weblogs. The lists provided below are necessarily selective rather than comprehensive; new resources are appearing all the time.

Printed sources

This list includes printed books, plus articles in professional and technical journals and magazines. It does not include the many articles in newspapers and popular magazines, in part because these articles may be difficult for many readers to access.

Books

Bausch, Paul, Matthew Haughey and Meg Hourihan. *We Blog: Publishing Online with Weblogs*. Indianapolis, IN: Wiley, 2002.

Blood, Rebecca. *The Weblog Handbook: Practical Advice on Creating and Maintaining Your Blog*. Cambridge, MA: Perseus Publishing, 2002.

Chromatic, Brian Aker and David Krieger. *Running Weblogs With Slash*. Sebastopol, CA: O'Reilly, 2002.

Hammersley, Ben. *Content Syndication With RSS*. London: O'Reilly UK, 2003.

Powers, Shelley, Cory Doctorow, J. Scott Johnson, Mena G. Trott and Benjamin Trott. *Essential Blogging*. Sebastopol, CA: O'Reilly, 2002.

Salam Pax. *Salam Pax: The Clandestine Diary of an Ordinary Iraqi*. New York: Grove Press, 2003.

Stauffer, Todd. *Blog On: Building Online Communities With Web Logs*. New York: McGraw-Hill/Osborne, 2003.

Stone, Biz. *Blogging: Genius Strategies for Instant Web Content*. Indianapolis, IN: New Riders, 2002.

We've Got Blog: How Weblogs Are Changing Our Culture, intro. Rebecca Blood. Cambridge, MA: Perseus Publishing, 2002.

Articles

Balas, Janet. 'Here a Blog, There a Blog, Even the Library Has a Web Log', *Computers in Libraries* 23.10 (2003): 41–43.

Barron, Daniel B. 'Blogs, Wikis, Alt Com, and the New Information Landscape: A Library Media Specialist's Guide', *School Library Media Activities Monthly* 20.2 (2003): 48–51.

Berger, Pam. 'Are You Blogging Yet?', *Information Searcher* 14.2 (2003): 1–4.

Block, Marylaine. 'Communicating Off the Page: Librarian-Created Web Zines and Weblogs', *Library Journal* 26.15 (2001): 50–52.

Clyde, Laurel A. 'Weblogs Go to School', *Access* 6.2 (2002): 17–20.

Clyde, Laurel A. 'Shall We Blog?', *Teacher Librarian* 30.1 (2002): 44–46.

Cohen, Steven M. 'Using RSS: An Explanation and Guide', *Information Outlook* 6.12 (2002): 6–10.

Crawford, Walt. '"You Must Read This": Library Weblogs', *American Libraries* 32.9 (2001): 74–76.

D'Aguiar, Hazel. 'Weblogs: The New Internet Community?', *CILIP Update* 2.1 (2003): 38–39.

Embrey, Theresa Ross. 'You Blog, We Blog: A Guide to How Teacher-Librarians Can Use Weblogs to Build Communications and Research Skills', *Teacher Librarian* 30.2 (2002): 7–9.

French, Bill. 'French Window: Emergent Publishing', *Information Age* Apr./May 2002: 10–11.

Goans, Doug and Teri M. Vogel. 'Building a Home for Library News With a Blog', *Computers in Libraries* 23.10 (2003): 20–26.

Harder, Geoffrey and Randy Reichardt. 'Throw Another Blog on the "Wire": Librarians and the Weblogging Phenomena', *Feliciter* 49.2 (2003): 85–88.

Horrocks, Nigel. '15 Minutes of Fame', *Australian Net-Guide* Sep. 2003: 20–27.

Huwe, Terence K. 'Born to Blog', *Computers in Libraries* 23.10 (2003): 44–45.

Mattison, Dave. 'So You Want to Start a Syndicated Revolution: RSS News Blogging for Searchers', *Searcher* 11.2 (2003): 38–48.

Stone, Steven A. 'The Library Blog: A New Communication Tool', *Kentucky Libraries* 67.4 (2003): 14–15.

Tennant, Roy. 'Feed Your Head: Keeping Up by Using RSS', *Library Journal* 15 May 2003: 30.

Wilson, Paula. 'Digital Librarian's Professional Reading Shelf: Magazines, Web Sites, Electronic Discussion Groups, and Weblogs', *Public Libraries* 41.4 (2002): 207–208.

Internet-based sources

Included in this list are specialist websites and individual pages, plus articles in online journals and magazines.

Specialist websites or pages

The Evolution of RSS (Andrew King)

http://www.webreference.com/authoring/languages/xml/rss/1/

Explanation of RSS, How You Can Use It, and Finding RSS Feeds (Michael Fagan)

http://www.faganfinder.com/search/rss.shtml

RSS – A Primer for Publishers and Content Providers (M. Moffat, EEVL)

http://www.eevl.ac.uk/rss_primer/

RSS Readers (Peter Scott)

http://www.lights.com/weblogs/rss.html

Weblog Compendium (Peter Scott)

http://www.lights.com/weblogs/

Weblogs (Laurel A. Clyde)

http://www.hi.is/~anne/weblogs.html

Weblogs, Journals and RSS (Michael Fagan)

http://www.faganfinder.com/blogs/

Articles

Blood, Rebecca. 'Weblogs: A History and Perspective', *Rebecca's Pocket* 7 Sep. 2000. Online (available at *http:// www.rebeccablood.net/essays/weblog_history.html* accessed 15 Apr. 2002).

Carver, Blake. 'Is It Time to Get Blogging?', *Library Journal* 15 Jan. 2003. Online (available at *http://www .libraryjournal.com/index.asp?layout=article&articleid= CA266428* accessed 26 Mar. 2004).

Clyde, Laurel A. 'Weblogs and Blogging, Part 1', *Free Pint* 111, 2 May 2002. Online (available at *http://www .freepint.com/issues/020502.htm#feature* accessed 7 Sep. 2003).

Clyde, Laurel A. 'Weblogs and Blogging, Part 2', *Free Pint* 112, 16 May 2002. Online (available at *http://www .freepint.com/issues/160502.htm* accessed 7 Sep. 2003).

Cohen, Steven M. 'RSS for Non-Techie Librarians', *LLRX.com* 3 Jun. 2002. Online (available at *http://www .llrx.com/features/rssforlibrarians.html* accessed 5 Apr. 2003).

Cook, Jason. 'Sharing Your Site With RSS', *Webmonkey* 14 May 2003. Online (available at *http://hotwired.lycos.com/ webmonkey/03/17/index3a.html* accessed 15 Apr. 2003).

Cowen, Amy. 'Blogging Goes Mobile', *mpulse magazine* Aug. 2003. Online (available at *http://www.cooltown .com/mpulse/0803-mblogging.asp* accessed 8 Sep. 2003).

Fowler, Geoffrey A. '... Find a Blog', *The Wall Street Journal Online* 18 Nov. 2002. Online (available at *http://www.waxy.org/random/html/wsj_findablog.html* accessed 15 Dec. 2002).

Howell, Denise M. 'Law Meets Blog: Electronic Publishing Comes of Age', *LLRX.com* 1 May 2002. Online (available at *http://www.llrx.com/features/lawblog.htm* accessed 4 May 2002).

McIntosh, Neil. 'A Tale of One Man and his Blog', *The Guardian*, 31 Jan. 2002. Online (available at *http://www.guardian.co.uk/online/story/0,3605,641742,00.html* accessed 15 Apr. 2002).

Manjoo, Farhad. 'Blah, Blah, Blah and Blog', *Wired* 18 Feb. 2002. Online (available at *http://www.wired.com/news/culture/0,1284,50443,00.html* accessed 15 Mar. 2002).

Miller, P. 'Syndicated Content: More Than Just File Formats?', *Ariadne* 25, 2003. Online (available at *http://www.ariadne.ac.uk/issue35/miller/* accessed 5 Sep. 2003).

Richardson, Will. 'Blogging and RSS – The "What's It?" and "How to" of Powerful New Web Tools for Educators', *MultiMedia Schools* 11.1 (2004). Online (available at *http://www.infotoday.com/MMSchools/jan04/richardson.shtml* accessed 1 Mar. 2004).

'RSS: Your Gateway to News and Blog Content', *Search Engine Watch* 2 Apr. 2003. Online (available at *http://www.searchenginewatch.com/sereport/article.php/2175281* accessed 18 Apr. 2003).

Shirky, Clay. 'Weblogs and the Mass Amateurization of Publishing' 2002. Online (available at *http://www.shirky.com/writings/weblogs_publishing.html* accessed 5 Sep. 2003).

Schwartz, Greg. 'Blogs for Libraries', *WebJunction* 3 Aug. 2003. Online (available at *http://www.webjunction.org/do/DisplayContent?id=1432* accessed 8 Sep. 2003).

Stone, Biz. 'Labs, Robots and Giant Floating Brains: The Amazingly True Story of Blogger!', *Webreview* 9 Mar. 2001. Online (available at *http://www.webreview.com/2001/03_09/strategists/index02.shtml* accessed 15 Apr. 2002).

Weblogs about weblogs and blogging

Just as the Internet is an important source of information about the Internet, so weblogs are an important source of information about weblogs and blogging.

The Blog Herald

http://www.blogherald.com/

Blogroots

http://www.blogroots.com/

Corante Tech News, Filtered Daily

http://www.corante.com/

LIS Blogsource: The Library Weblog About Library Weblogs

http://lisblogsource.net/

Weblogs: About Weblog Technology and Usage

http://radio.weblogs.com/0105673/categories/weblog/

Index

Printed in the United States
40380LVS00003B/48